MW00806232

Worship and

Wonder

Faith-Filled Devotions

Love & Blessings,
Tracy ♡

By Tracy Hill

© 2021 by Tracy Hill

All rights reserved. Except as provided by the Copyright Act no part of this publication may be reproduced, stored in a retrieval system or transmitted in any form or by any means without the prior written permission of the publisher.

Cover photographs copyright © Tracy Hill 2021. All rights reserved.

Cover designs by Camden Hill, copyright © 2018. Used by permission. All rights reserved.

All Scripture quotations, unless otherwise indicated, are taken from the Holy Bible, New International Version®, NIV®. Copyright ©1973, 1978, 1984, 2011 by Biblica, Inc.™ Used by permission of Zondervan. All rights reserved worldwide. www.zondervan.com, The "NIV" and "New International Version" are trademarks registered in the United States Patent and Trademark Office by Biblica, Inc.™

Certain noted Scripture quotations are from the ESV® Bible (The Holy Bible, English Standard Version®), copyright © 2001 by Crossway, a publishing ministry of Good News Publishers. Used by permission. All rights reserved.

Scriptures marked NKJV are taken from the New King James Version (NKJV): Scripture taken from the New King James Version®. Copyright© 1982 by Thomas Nelson, Inc. Used by permission. All rights reserved.

ISBN: 978-0-9976913-5-1

Dedicated to...

Russell, my wonderful husband; my best friend.

I am so grateful for you!

Welcome!

I am so delighted to have you join me on this amazing journey of faith! Most of the pages within this little book were written during the year-long pandemic of 2020 and the first half of 2021. I find it so appropriate that the world emerged from quarantine just in time to greet the Spring. As flowers sprung from the ground, people emerged from their houses. As birds took to the sky, the earth once again came alive with the joyous sound of people gathering. As leaves unfurled to soak up the sun, people relished their new lease on life. Much of what I have penned was inspired by the Lord's faithfulness to me, and to all His people. Although the world often seemed to have lost its marbles, evidence of God's goodness and control were visible all around. I walked through this period of time much as I always have—overcome by the Lord's sovereignty and love. God is good all the time, even amid all the bad. He is the Anchor for my soul through any storm; He is the solid Rock on which my feet stand. When I contemplate His glory, I cannot help but be filled with awe and wonder; I am compelled to worship His Holy Name.

Throughout this devotional, you and I will meditate on God's lavish love. We will be overcome with wonder at His awesome holiness and power. We will be humbled before Him in reverent praise and worship. Every page is filled with inspiration meant to remind us of our blessings and encourage and grow our faith. You will find prayer prompts and questions to help you internalize the messages in your own heart and life.

I pray that you encounter the Lord in a fresh new way through the devotions and the Scriptures that follow.

I hope that you are abundantly blessed and inspired! XOXO Tracy

Interlaced

The posture of *worship* and the heart of *wonder* are like fingers beautifully interlaced—they joyfully go hand-in-hand and are lovingly bound together. The word *worship* signifies an attitude of reverence, adoration, devotion, praise, and honor. In respect to our relationship with God, it signifies a heart of complete surrender, shown through the action of our bowing down to Him as Lord and Savior. The posture of worship cannot be faked, it must flow from a personal encounter with Jesus. It comes from standing in His Presence and gazing at His beautiful face; it comes from getting to know Him personally and realizing He holds the world is in His capable hands. Overcome with *wonder* at His majesty and power, enraptured by His love and grace, caught up in all His glory, we cannot help but fall to our knees or lift our hands in complete adoration. Our worship of God flows effortlessly from a place of awestruck wonder.

Psalm 29:2, "Ascribe to the LORD the glory due his name; worship the LORD in the splendor of his holiness."

How does the majesty of the Lord cause you to worship and wonder?

When I look around me at His beautiful creation The mountains, birds, bunnies, and squirrels. I praise Him for it.

If you need more space for writing and responding to the prompts, there are blank pages at the end of the book just waiting for you to fill them. (pg. 175)

Spirit and Truth

We come to God and worship Him on His terms, not ours. He is the One who designed every intricate detail about us, and He created this world according to His perfect order. He has always had a plan and a purpose for everything in heaven above and here on earth below, including our salvation through His only Begotten Son. God did not leave us to grasp in the darkness and to figure things out on our own. In His sovereignty, He has appointed just one way into His Holy Presence. He has given us His Truth to lead the way, and His Spirit to guide us home. We come to God and worship Him through Jesus Christ, alone. When we open God's Word, His Holy Spirit is the One who brings it to life in us, confirming the truth about Jesus that we have read.

John 4:24, "God is spirit, and his worshipers must worship in the Spirit and in truth."

Ask for the Holy Spirit to bring God's Word alive in your life, making it more than mere words on a page, but having the power to revive your soul.

Holy Spirit awaken my by the truth of God's Word make the Word alive to me. I just dont want to read it like a book. Give me rhema wood that cycles through my mind into the fertile soil of my heart. Let it your word take root in the fertile soil of my heart. Give me the spirit of wisdom and revelation to grow in the knowledge of the beauty of Jesus and God's personality. In Jesus name Amen.

Waiting

Worship and waiting are two essential components to a faith-filled life. Worship is ascribing all glory, honor, and praise to our worthy and faithful Lord. Worship entails not just our songs, but encompasses our thoughts, words, and actions. We worship the Lord by surrendering and offering up every aspect of our lives. Worship declares that we believe God is who He says He is! Worship is also found in our waiting on the Lord. Waiting affirms our faith and trust in God's goodness. Waiting quietly proclaims that we believe God's ways and timing to be best. Waiting says, "not my will, but Yours be done; not on my schedule, but on Your timetable Lord." It says, "I trust You Lord to show me Your path at the perfect time, and until that moment I will be still and rest."

Lord, let my life be a testimony to Your incredible goodness. May both my actions and stillness give glory to You. Help me to live out my faith with *worship and waiting*. Amen.

Isaiah 26:8, "Yes, LORD, walking in the way of your laws, we wait for you; your name and renown are the desire of our hearts."

What do you need to wait on God for today? Ask Him to help you trust His timing.

Heart Matter

Worship is more than acting righteous and quoting the Bible word for word; it is more than knowing the difference between right and wrong; it is more than rule following and looking good to those around. Worship, at its core, is a matter of the heart. We can say and do all the right things but still be far from God. An authentic and intimate relationship and a surrendered and honest heart is what the Lord is after. Our human knowledge, wisdom, and intellect will only bring us so far in knowing about God. Yet our hearts are what teach us about who He really is and draw us to know Him deeply and personally. He is not some far off unapproachable deity; He is our Lord, our Savior, our Father, our Friend. Let us worship and adore Him and approach Him as such.

Isaiah 29:13-14, "The Lord says: 'These people come near to me with their mouth and honor me with their lips, but their hearts are far from me. Their worship of me is based on merely human rules they have been taught. Therefore once more I will astound these people with wonder upon wonder; the wisdom of the wise will perish, the intelligence of the intelligent will vanish.'"

Reflect on the freedom you have of approaching God from your heart and not through rules and regulations.

Grace

I believe that *grace* is the most beautiful word in the human language. If *grace* were a flower, it would be a rose whose fragrance lingers in the air and permeates the garden. If *grace* were a food, it would be dripping with the sweetness of honey.

Grace is a demonstration of all that is good and pure in the world. It is the salvation of the LORD revealed to mankind through His Son, Jesus Christ. Grace embodies the character and actions of God toward His children every day—it blesses the undeserved and sees value in every individual. Grace searches for the lost and it comforts those who are hurting. Grace loves the unlovable and it forgives those who do the trespassing. Grace permits room for change and it hopes for godly transformation; it allows for mistakes and celebrates any progress made in the Lord's direction. Grace invites us to take our place at the table when we haven't earned a seat. Grace sets the captive free; it is the place of forgiveness and fresh beginnings. Grace helps us to see the best in others with the same grace-filled perspective through which the Lord views us. Grace always points us to our Heavenly Father, and it graciously leads us in His righteous way of Truth.

The word *grace* brings a smile to my face. God's outpouring of *grace* brings peace to my heart. My act of *grace* brings God's compassion to our world.

Grace—there is no sweeter word ever spoken.

John 1:16, "Out of His fullness we have all received grace in place of grace already given."

What does the word *grace* mean to you?

The Cross

The small wooden cross on the cover of this book is a precious souvenir that I brought home from the Holy Land of Israel. The cross is crafted from the wood of an olive tree, which grow in abundance throughout the country. This cross serves as a reminder of all that Jesus suffered for me. His death brought me eternal life and a restored relationship with my Heavenly Father. Knowing all that His sacrifice would accomplish, Jesus considered it joy to give His life for you and me. With our eyes firmly fixed on Jesus, it becomes our joy to surrender our lives in order to follow Him. With the Cross in mind, we throw off sin, shame, doubt, insecurities, fears, worries, and discouragements; and we run with wondrous abandon toward Jesus. The Cross changes everything for you and me. It is the key to God's Heavenly Kingdom!

Hebrews 12:1-3, "Therefore, since we are surrounded by such a great cloud of witnesses, let us throw off everything that hinders and the sin that so easily entangles. And let us run with perseverance the race marked out for us, fixing our eyes on Jesus, the pioneer and perfecter of faith. For the joy set before him he endured the cross, scorning its shame, and sat down at the right hand of the throne of God. Consider him who endured such opposition from sinners, so that you will not grow weary and lose heart."

What does the Cross mean to you?

A New Name

When the children of God pass away from this earth and enter eternity, all their cares of this world pass away too. The ways of the world no longer have hold over them; they are completely set free of everything that held them captive. They are freed from the imperfect and temporary trappings, the ailments and pain, the confusion and struggles, the sin and shame. They are held in the arms of our Savior and finally realize eternal perfection. They forever reside in the Kingdom of Heaven where love, peace, and righteousness reign, where they are given a new body and a new authority and purpose, represented by a brand-new name.

Revelation 2:17, "To the one who is victorious, I will give some of the hidden manna. I will also give that person a white stone with a new name written on it, known only to the one who receives it."

How does the promise of all this *newness* impact your life with hope today?

Vessel

I am the Lord's vessel. Before the day even begins, I ask Him to ready my heart and clear my mind and fill me with His Holy Spirit. I pray to be His useful instrument, sharing His love all around; spreading His mercy and grace as I go through my day. I humbly ask God to use me to bless others—both through my words and my actions. I know if I listen, He will tell me what to say. He will show me who needs a helping hand or a simple word of encouragement. I can be used as God's blessing, so long as I do not stumble over myself and I stay out of my own way. I am His vessel, His instrument of peace; I do nothing of eternal value on my own, it is God who gets the praise.

2 Corinthians 4:7, "But we have this treasure in earthen vessels, that the excellence of the power may be of God and not of us."

2 Timothy 2:21, "Those who cleanse themselves from the latter will be instruments for special purposes, made holy, useful to the Master and prepared to do any good work."

How can you prepare and offer yourself to be used as God's holy vessel and instrument today?

Assured

Step out on God's Word and believe. Walk in faith and walk assuredly on the surface of the water. Keep your eyes on the Savior and do the impossible—inch by inch, one foot at a time, or by leaps and bounds.

Faith trusts in the goodness of God and believes that His Promises to us are true. Faith sees the possible even in seemingly impossible situations. Faith believes that God is exponentially bigger than all of our problems. Faith chooses to move forward, marching out of the confines of fear. Faith keeps its eyes on Jesus, follows His call, and steps out of the boat. Faith is the assurance that Jesus will catch us if we fall. Faith moves mountains and throws them into the sea. Faith is delightfully contagious and grows like a mustard seed. It believes God's Word over all the other voices we hear.

Faith does not toil and spin, worry and fret, stress out and react poorly, or lead to regret. Faith trusts God to meet all our needs and to clothe us properly and beautifully in garments of salvation and praise.

Faith is confident that the Lord is steadfast and trustworthy; faith is assured in the hope that His Promises bring. Faith calls us to be brave, and bold, and beautifully confident. Faith reminds us to be gentle and humble, and loving and kind.

Faith rests in the knowledge that above all else, we are God's beloved children, and we have a heavenly inheritance in store.

Hebrews 11:1, "Now faith is confidence in what we hope for and assurance about what we do not see."

Praise God and thank Him for His faithfulness. Ask Him to help you move forward in assurance today.

Write out your prayer here:

Dear God,

Amen.

Blessed

God pours out continual blessings on those He loves. He withholds no good thing from those who love Him in return. A relationship with Jesus will never leave us lacking. Insurmountable amounts of joy, hope, peace, and love are always at our disposal. He has blessed us with everything we could possibly need for living out our faith while we dwell here on earth. He blesses us with strength for the times we need to persevere. He blesses us with courage when our circumstances would otherwise demand we succumb to fear. He blesses us with faith to move mountains and overcome obstacles that are in our way; He blesses us with His wisdom for traversing this world, and discernment in choosing our best path forward. God blesses us with a knowledge of His will, and an awareness of His Presence with us. He blesses us with His Holy Word, as written in the Bible, and with His very own Holy Spirit to reside in our hearts. God has indeed blessed us abundantly with every spiritual blessing in the heavenly realms that we could possibly dream of.

Ephesians 1:3, "Praise be to the God and Father of our Lord Jesus Christ, who has blessed us in the heavenly realms with every spiritual blessing in Christ."

Pause and thank God for giving you every heavenly spiritual blessing you could possibly need as you live here on earth.

Stayed

Faith, trust, focus and peace all go harmoniously hand-in-hand.

Circumstances and people do not have to dictate whether we have peace or not. Peace is available to us apart from these, if only we would choose to lay hold of it. Peace is attainable by focusing our eyes on God, by redirecting our minds onto His Word, and filling our hearts with the knowledge of His extravagant love. Peace washes over us when we meditate on God's promises, His faithfulness, and His goodness.

Even when things are in chaos and life seems out of sorts, peace is possible still. The peace of God within us is not circumstantial; it is rooted, anchored, and built on who we know our Heavenly Father to be—He is good and perfect, righteous and just, kind and merciful, gracious and loving beyond belief. He is mighty and powerful, awesome and great. He is personal and intimately close-up. Peace is found when we reflect on God's character and remember His enduring Presence throughout our lives; and when we trust that His plans for us are unequivocally good. Even when we do not see clearly or understand what God is up to, we can assuredly believe and trust that it is something extraordinary. In this way, peace that surpasses all our human understanding becomes ours to claim. When we trust God and our focus is stayed on Him, peace then becomes our restful state of mind.

Isaiah 26:3, "You will keep in perfect peace those whose minds are steadfast, because they trust in you."

How do you notice the correlation between your faith and peace?

The Beginning

If we want wisdom, we must first and foremost start with an awestruck, reverent fear of the Lord—that is the solid foundation on which we are to build our lives. God is terrifying, big, capable, awesome, holy, and powerful, unable to tolerate sin of any kind, yet out of love for humanity He withholds His wrath and pours out salvation through Jesus Christ. Out of mercy He takes our punishment on the Cross, and out of lavish grace He gives us the forgiveness we do not deserve. Knowing the judgement that God could have unleashed and experiencing His amazing gift of grace in its place should cause us to drop to our knees and bow our grateful heads. Fear of the Lord is not the dreaded end, but the gloriously hope-filled beginning.

Proverbs 1:7, "The fear of the LORD is the beginning of knowledge, but fools despise wisdom and instruction."

How does an awestruck, wondrous fear of the Lord impact the way you receive His salvation, read His Word, and approach His Heavenly Throne?

Believing

I know what God has done; I believe what God can do.

Nothing spurs our faith onward more than meditating on the truth of these two statements. Looking back, if we have paid any attention, we have seen the powerful hand of God move in our lives—sometimes through little blessings and other times through mighty miracles of which only He could possibly do. Reflecting on the past workings of God gives us faith for the present, and hope for the coming days. Any time doubts or fears try to settle in and take over, push them aside by recounting God's faithfulness, taking Him at His Word, and believing Him for your future. God meets our belief with His mighty action.

Matthew 8:13, "Then Jesus said to the centurion, "Go! Let it be done just as you believed it would." And his servant was healed at that moment."

What has God already done in your life? What do you believe He can do in your life presently?

Closer

From all the living I have done thus far, I know that life with Jesus is the absolute best! He tells us to seek His Face, pursue His ways, and trust Him for all the rest.

There is no looking back with shame or regret; no worrying or wallowing the present away. He calls you and me to something much better—a life filled with hope, peace, and joy as we trust Him to hold our future. He is our way forward, one step at a time; grab hold of His hand and walk in His shadow, following closely and confidently alongside Him.

Nothing in this world is beyond God's knowledge or grasp; it is all laid out before Him. He knows the path ahead, before it even unfolds before us. He knows the obstacles and hurdles, the dangers and pitfalls, the mountaintops and valleys, the joys and sorrows, and everything else that awaits us. He will show us what to avoid and carry us through the unavoidable, as we keep forging ahead with Him.

He knows the deepest longings of our hearts and He shows us the best way forward, which is always in the direction of being closer to Him. God's way always leads us to the very best He has to offer. He leads us to Himself—there is no better place to be.

Psalm 16:11, *"You make known to me the path of life; you will fill me with joy in your presence, with eternal pleasures at your right hand."*

How have you personally found God's way to be the best way?

In the Fullness

Grace: unmerited favor

Lord, I pray that Your grace would come alive in my heart and overflow as peace in my life. May Your grace spring from my lips in spontaneous worship; may it cause my hands to reach toward the heavens in awe and cause me to humbly fall to my knees in reverence. May Your grace fill my heart with praise; may it alter the way I look at life and the way I view other people. May Your grace inspire words of kindness to roll off my tongue and be the guard which keeps my lips from speaking harm. May Your amazing grace inspire me to be amazingly gracious even to those who offend me. May I go the extra mile and lay down my life in sacrifice, just as You did for me. You grace is sufficient for all my needs—it bridges the distance between God and me, and it bridges the gap in all my relationships. Your grace is sufficient in bringing me peace, both in my relationship with You and in my relationships with others.

Thank You for the gift of grace, and for Your gracious example. Help me to live in the fullness of Your grace and receive the resulting peace. Help me to pass it on to everyone I encounter.

Amen.

1 Corinthians 1:3, *"Grace and peace to you from God our Father and the Lord Jesus Christ."*

Is there an area of your life where you need to receive the fullness of God's grace? An area where you need to give it?

Bountiful

(This devotion was written midway through Covid quarantine.) After six months of lock-down and social distancing it does not take much to excite me. This morning I took a trip to the local farmer's market with my husband and our younger son who was home for the weekend. These days any trip out of the house seems almost as adventurous as a trip across the country or a jaunt around the globe. Seeing other humans face-to-face, even if at a distance, is a remarkable event on its own. Fresh air (actually quite smoky due to the California fires), blue sky (maybe more of a gray hue), a drive around town through the bustling roadways (a few cars count as traffic these days)—despite these less than favorable conditions it was a joy to be out and about. The dull skies did nothing to dampen our spirits—we strolled the aisles of the farmer's market, our eyes drawn to the vibrant colors of fresh vegetables and fruits; the smell of herbs and flowers wafting by; the vendors pleasantly smiling, their mouths obscured behind their masks, but at least you could see their cheery eyes.

Bountiful blessings joyously lurk around every corner, and abundant blessings pop out at every turn. They are waiting for us to take notice and discover their unexpected presence all around. Blessings do not have to come in large packages, they are just as sweet in blueberry size.

Psalm 106:1, "Praise the LORD. Give thanks to the LORD, for he is good; his love endures forever."

Dull skies or bright blue, give thanks to the Lord for the blessings He pours out today.

Breath

Raise your hand if you have a birthday this year. What a coincidence, I do too! Birthdays are wonderful because they focus on celebrating one special person for a whole special day. Birthdays commemorate the day we entered this huge wide world and God gave us our very first breath. Birthday anniversaries come along once a year, and on that one day, we get to use our breath to blow up balloons and blow out the candles on our delicious and colorfully decorated cake. Birthdays are a big occasion to rejoice and thank God for giving us life. Besides our physical birthday, we have another amazing reason to rejoice and give thanks—the day of our spiritual rebirth! Jesus said that in order to enter the Kingdom of God and Heaven, we must be born again. Fortunately, the moment we said *"yes!"* to Jesus, He gave us new and eternal life by breathing His Holy Spirit into our very souls!

Let us recount the miracles of our lives: God gave us breath on the day of our birth; He gives us breath to fill our lungs every morning that we are blessed enough to wake up and open our eyes. He gives us the breath of His Holy Spirit to revive our spirits and secure the salvation of our souls; He grants us access to freely join Him in Paradise. Now each of these things on its own is enough reason to rejoice, but add them all together and that is something quite extraordinary to commemorate and celebrate!

Psalm 150:6, *"Let everything that has breath praise the LORD. Praise the LORD."*

With the next breath we take, let us also praise God and give Him thanks!

Just Believe

It is such a huge relief to know that I do not have to earn my way into Heaven; I do not have to work for my salvation. I do not have to be perfect before God to wants to begin a relationship with me. I must simply believe in Jesus and receive His extravagant, no-strings-attached, free gift of grace. He lifts the burden of inadequacy and insufficiency from my shoulders. He fills in the gaps of my flaws and my failures. The moment I place my faith in Jesus, God receives me as I am and makes me His child. After I am already secure in His Hands, my Heavenly Father begins the tender process of helping me more closely resemble Him. He is the one who will remake me into the best version of myself.

John 1:12, "Yet to all who did receive Him, to those who believed in His name, He gave the right to become children of God—"

Describe the relief you have in knowing that you do not need to earn God's love and that you can't lose your place in His family.

Bright Spot

Even among the tangled brambles of life there are bright spots to be found. Though life can be hard and sometimes quite prickly, there are delightful glimpses of beauty blooming all around. If we stop all our striving and wrestling for a moment, and simply come to the Lord, He will gladly reveal those glimpses to us. As I am writing these words it is dawning on me, all the bright spots that Jesus points out along our path are directing us right back to Him—He, Himself is the real Bright Spot we long and search for in the course of our thorny, knotted-up lives.

Zephaniah 3:17, "The LORD your God in your midst, The Mighty One, will save; He will rejoice over you with gladness, He will quiet you with His love, He will rejoice over you with singing." NKJV

Take a moment to reflect on all the bright spots God has placed in your life. (Look closely, they are there.) How do they point you to Jesus, the brightest spot of all?

Brilliance

On a recent trip to Israel, the group I was traveling with stayed a couple of nights in a hotel on the shore of the Sea of Galilee. Walking back to my room on one of the evenings, I noticed that the whole region was pitch black except for the ancient town of Tiberius which was built into a hillside and sparkled brilliantly in the distance. In contrast to the darkness, the lights of the town shone brightly and were visible from miles around. Although modern electricity illuminates the homes and streets today, the candles flickering in the windows two thousand years ago would have put on their own spectacular display.

This is the place where Jesus spoke these words from Matthew 5:13-14, *"You are the light of the world. A town built on a hill cannot be hidden."*

Much like the city of Tiberius, we are called to be *like a city on a hill*, a beacon of hope to everyone around, much like the breaking dawn giving light to a brand-new day. We are to be like stars shining in the night sky, helping others find their course and navigate their journey. Amid the darkness of this world, we are meant to shine brightly for all to see, lighting the way to Jesus, the source of all hope, love, and peace.

Philippians 2:15, "so that you may become blameless and pure, children of God without fault in a warped and crooked generation. Then you will shine among them like stars in the sky..."

How can you shine brilliantly for Jesus today?

Captive

Sometimes I just don't know what to think—my mind runs wild with questions of *What if? Why? How? When?* These uncertain thoughts and doubts cause a great deal of anxiety. They lead me astray, down rabbit trails where I was never meant to wander. They lead me along winding paths and blow me aimlessly at the wind's command and whim.

Lord, You tell me to take my thoughts captive and make them obedient to You. You tell me to knock, ask, and seek for Your will to be done in my life. You ask me to trust in Your plans, Your timing, Your ways. You remind me that Your purposes for me are perfect and good. Lord, help me to obey Your prompting and turn my thoughts over to You. Help me to stop striving and stressing, and instead rest in Your care and draw peace from Your Presence. Help me to trust in Your power and follow the path that You have laid out. Taking my thoughts captive and making them obedient to You is the surest and quickest route to mental clarity and freedom. Thank you for encouraging me toward this graciously liberating option. Amen.

2 Corinthians 10:5, *"We demolish arguments and every pretension that sets itself up against the knowledge of God, and we take captive every thought to make it obedient to Christ."*

What thoughts do you need to take captive and turn over to the Lord? I urge you to do so now.

A Command

Jesus tells us that the world will know we are His disciples by the uniqueness of our love for one another; not by our songs of worship, not by our righteousness, not by our thorough knowledge of Scripture. Although these practices are a vital part of a Christian's life, they ultimately are not what draws others to their Savior. Only the love of God flowing through our lives can do something so powerful as that. Everyone needs love, everyone desires love. When people feel loved they listen. Love has the greatest impact of all.

Scripture plainly tells us that unless the signature of our lives is love, all our preaching and praising will be in vain and sound much like *a resounding gong or a clanging cymbal*. (1 Corinthians 13:1)

We are commanded over and over again to love, not only those whom we agree with, but those we would rather not even associate with. Love is the glorious and holy standard that Jesus calls us to pursue in representing Him accurately and well. Love is the basis by which we should judge our words and actions towards others in this world. Love should give us pause before opening our mouths and closing off doors. Jesus came from Heaven in pursuit of imperfect sinners—people just like you and me—and He gave His life in the fullest expression of sacrificial love, despite our depravity. He did not come to judge us, but rather to love us into His Family, and He commands us to love others sacrificially in His Name.

Love must be the obvious signature of our lives—our worship must be infused and overflowing with praise and love for God; our righteousness should be spurred on by a love for God's ways; our knowledge of the Bible propelled by a love for God's Words.

But to reach others with the Gospel Message, a love for others must pave the way. Love softens hearts, it breaks down walls, it removes barriers, and opens ears. Love reveals Jesus most authentically.

Here are a few questions to help us assess our hearts and attitudes before speaking or engaging with others: *"Am I reacting on selfish impulse or in hateful retribution, or responding in selfless Christ-like love? Am I representing Jesus well? Would He be pleased with me? Am I obeying His command to love others?"* How we answer these questions directs the course of our lives and impacts the lives of others as well. Our behavior has the power to lead people to seek the Savior, or push them further away.

Let's live for Jesus and love others extravagantly in His Name.

John 13:34-35, ""A new command I give you: Love one another. As I have loved you, so you must love one another. By this everyone will know that you are my disciples, if you love one another."

How does knowing that love is not an option change the way you approach and respond to people? Who can you share Jesus' love with? Ask the Lord to help you represent Him well.

Child of God

Who am I?

How we answer this question will largely determine the trajectory of our lives.

If we view ourselves merely as human beings existing on this planet for a certain length of time, our hope will be shortsighted, and we will never be completely satisfied. We will exhaust ourselves, grasping at every last moment, seeking to prolong our days, afraid to let go and face what's down the road.

If we see ourselves as just a creature of habit trying to get by and simply surviving, the joy and the blessings of this life will escape us. We will forget to stop and smell the roses, the lilies, and the lilacs and miss their intoxicating fragrance.

If our identity is wrapped up in our perfection, our work, or achievements, then the real purpose and beauty of our life will be lost on us. If we are incessantly striving and pouring all our energy and time into keeping up appearances, we'll find ourselves on a self-esteem roller coaster. Our confidence will wane anytime we fall short of our own expectations.

If our identity is wrapped up in being a wife, a mother, a daughter, a friend, and those roles and relationships alter and change, or even disintegrate, we may feel as if we have lost our sense of identity too.

If our identity is held captive to pain, shame, and regret from the past, we will miss out on the gift of the present because we refuse to step out of our chains.

If we find our identity in any of the answers above, we will at some point find ourselves feeling empty, discontented, disillusioned, or forgotten. The movement of our lives will be too fast, at a complete standstill, or headed in the wrong direction.

If on the other hand our identity is found in our relationship with God, our glorious Creator, then our outlook on all the above roles and identities will take on a new light. We no longer merely exist; we live, breathe, move with the hope of Christ alive in us. We no longer muddle through the mundane and routine—we find joy in the blessings both big and small that are waiting to be discovered all around us. We are no longer slaves to our work, trying to prove our worth. We work heartily, with joy, *as if working for the Lord*. We use our God-given strengths, talents, skills, and gifts to live out our purpose on earth while glorifying our Father in Heaven.

As a child of God our identity is secure and unchanging; we are loved and held by Him no matter what phase of life we are in. As a child of God, we have been set free. The prison doors have been thrown open—the shackles of sin, shame, unforgiveness, and fear of death have been broken.

If we find our identity in Christ and we align ourselves to Him, then the passage of our lives will be perfectly paced. We will move forward in grace, as we allow His rhythm to guide us. No longer looking down, or back, or too far forward, we will look up in hope, be filled with His peace, walk in His joy, pass on His love, and be motivated by faith. You and I are children of God.

John 1:12, "Yet to all who did receive him, to those who believed in his name, he gave the right to become children of God."

Where do you find your identity? Is it in the Lord? Is it as a child of God, safe and secure, valued and loved? I sure hope so!

Choose Jesus

I have found that without exception I am faced with choices every single day. I have also found that whatever possible scenarios come along throughout my waking hours, I must keep choosing Jesus. He alone is the Way.

When faced with worry, I must choose faith.

When faced with misery, I must choose joy.

When faced with despair, I must choose hope.

When faced with panic, I must choose peace.

When faced with bitterness, I must choose understanding.

When faced with regret, I must choose redemption.

When faced with grudges, I must choose forgiveness.

When faced with greed, I must choose generosity.

When faced with harshness, I must choose gentleness.

When faced with rudeness, I must choose kindness.

When faced with hate, I must choose love.

When faced with curses, I must choose blessing.

Jesus is the answer to every choice we face. Choose to love Him. Choose to seek Him. Choose to listen to His voice. Choose to persevere and persist, clinging tightly to Him with all your might. He is the way to truly abundant life.

Deuteronomy 30:19-20, "This day I call the heavens and the earth as witnesses against you that I have set before you life and death, blessings and curses. Now choose life, so that you and your children may live and that you may love the LORD your God, listen to his voice, and hold fast to him."

Personalize your own prayer to God in the space below.

Lord, help me to seek Your ways and choose You in this area of my life today:

Amen.

Well Up

Lord, we know that everything we need for an abundant life is found in You! You are the treasure we look and long for. We ask that You turn our ears to Your wisdom and open our eyes to Your holiness. Pierce our hearts with Your abundant love. Give us a revelation of who You are and what You desire from us. Impart to us a knowledge of Your righteousness and an understanding of Your will and Your ways. Instill in us a hunger to know You more deeply; give us a thirst for Your Life-Giving Word. Awaken in us the desire to pursue You and Your Kingdom with all our being. Well up within us an unsatiable longing for more of You. Help us to walk blameless and guard the course of our ways. In Jesus' Name we pray. Amen.

Proverbs 2:1-8, "My son, if you accept my words and store up my commands within you, turning your ear to wisdom and applying your heart to understanding—indeed, if you call out for insight and cry aloud for understanding, and if you look for it as for silver and search for it as for hidden treasure, then you will understand the fear of the LORD and find the knowledge of God. For the LORD gives wisdom; from his mouth come knowledge and understanding. He holds success in store for the upright, he is a shield to those whose walk is blameless, for he guards the course of the just and protects the way of his faithful ones."

Majesty

All of creation is crowned with God's glory. Every detail in heaven and on earth declares His holy majesty; none more loudly than His beloved children's lives. We are made in God's image and are created to worship the Lord and make known His Name.

If the stars, moon, and sun illuminate the sky and proclaim God's splendor, how much more should our lives? If every creature on this planet, both great and small, ascribes glory to the Lord, how much more should those who have been saved by His grace? We were created to worship the Lord in wonder, and praise His Majestic Name. It is the purpose for which we have been made.

Psalm 8:3-9, "When I consider your heavens, the work of your fingers, the moon and the stars, which you have set in place, what is mankind that you are mindful of them, human beings that you care for them? You have made them a little lower than the angels and crowned them with glory and honor. You made them rulers over the works of your hands; you put everything under their feet: all flocks and herds, and the animals of the wild, the birds in the sky, and the fish in the sea, all that swim the paths of the seas. Lord, our Lord, how majestic is your name in all the earth!"

How do you notice creation testify to God's majesty? How does your life reflect His glory?

Clarity

Getting an eye exam is quite an adventure—first they have you hold a big black spoon over each of your eyes and ask you to read the letters ranging from large to small that have been projected onto the illuminated wall in front of you. Then, your eyes are dilated with some drops that sting and after the medicine has had a chance to take effect, they place an awkward contraption in front of your face. You are asked to look through the lenses on the machine and choose which one helps your vision most. *"One or two?" "Two or one?"* Over and over again you are asked these questions until the correct lens suddenly brings everything into crisp focus, prompting you to alert the doctor to the lens that makes everything clear.

We all desire perfect vision—20/20 is the goal. Unfortunately, this is often not the case. The older I get the worse my close-up sight becomes, especially in the dark. I carry reading glasses in my purse and have pairs littered throughout the house. I need ready access to them, because seeing clearly is a blessing I truly appreciate.

Fortunately for us, a relationship with God will improve both our spiritual and mental vision above and beyond any other prescription. The more we get to know Him and the more time we spend diving into the Bible and on our knees in prayer, the sharper everything in our lives comes into focus. He gives us brand-new spectacles to see with His perspective. Looking back over our lives, our hindsight is enlightened as we see the Hand and Presence of God has been with us throughout. Standing in the present moment, the dim shadows fade, and the brilliance of God illuminates our way. Facing forward, being filled with hope in God's promises, our future suddenly becomes much brighter as if seeing in the light of day for the first time. God is the One who perfects our vision, adjusting our clarity and focus as we begin to see life through His eyes.

Let's praise the Lord for restoring our sight.

Luke 18:42-43, "Jesus said to him, "Receive your sight; your faith has healed you." Immediately he received his sight and followed Jesus, praising God. When all the people saw it, they also praised God."

How has Jesus restored your sight? How has He changed your perspective? Where could you use His perspective now?

Use this space to thank the Lord, or ask Him to help you receive your sight:

Community

Sure, dancing alone keeps others from stepping on your toes, but think of all the enjoyment you are missing out on. It's hard to Tango, Salsa, Cha Cha, Jive, Swing, or Waltz without someone else to twirl you around. You might not require a partner for line dancing, break dancing, or showing off your hip hop moves, but you will sure have a lot more fun if you do them in a group. You might get jostled, you might get bumped, but when all is said and done, the good far outweighs the bad. Likewise, living on our own may be the surest way to secure our safety, but an isolated Christian life is lacking in so many ways. God designed us to be in fellowship and community with other believers. There are so many benefits to be found when we step out of our comfort zone and reach out to those around, allowing them access to our hearts and lives. God designed the church in such a way that we all need each other to function properly—we spur each other on toward the full life Jesus intends for us to have. We encourage one another and keep each other on track; we come alongside each other and pray for one another's needs. There are so many blessings that come from being a part of the family of God. We all need community. God designed us this way.

Hebrews 10:24-25, "And let us consider how we may spur one another on toward love and good deeds, not giving up meeting together, as some are in the habit of doing, but encouraging one another—and all the more as you see the Day approaching."

How have you been encouraged by the family of God? How can you encourage a fellow believer?

Confident

Fear and faith are at odds with each other. They cannot harmoniously exist together for they are directly opposed in their purpose and function—one drags us down, the other builds us up; one stops us in our tracks, the other propels us onward. These rival forces war against each other and battle for our alliance, each desiring to control the state of our heart, mind, and soul. One wreaks havoc by directing our attention to our own weaknesses, while the other brings peace by reminding that God is in control. Fear is based on the perceived size of our situation; faith is based on the indisputable enormity of God. Absolutely nothing is bigger than God, of this we can be confident. Choosing to side with faith leaves no room for fear.

Psalm 27:3, "Though an army besiege me, my heart will not fear; though war break out against me, even then I will be confident."

Pray and ask God to help you overcome your fears with the power of faith. Ask Him to remind you that He is in control.

Every Bit

Lord, please clear my mind,

Calm my heart,

Strengthen my body,

And refresh my spirit.

Have your way with every bit of me.

Mold me and shape me,

From the inside and out,

Into the woman You want me to be.

My heart's desire is to glorify You,

With every bit of who I am.

Amen.

Isaiah 42:12, "Let the whole world glorify the LORD;

let it sing his praise."

Write out your own simple prayer of surrender here:

Endures

Seasons come and go,

Weather changes from warm to cold,

Flowers bloom then fade away.

Nothing on this planet ever stays the same,

But the faithfulness of the Lord

And the unshakable truth of His Word

Constantly and consistently remains unchanged.

Isaiah 40:8, "The grass withers and the flowers fall, but the word of

our God endures forever."

How does the unshakable truth of God's Word bring you stability and comfort?

Cookie Dough Comfort

I need Jesus every day, but occasionally I need some cookie dough too.

As young girl I often visited my grandparents, staying over for the weekend. My Grandma and I made chocolate chip cookies on almost every one of these occasions. I would sit on her teal blue stool and she would stand close by my side, handing me the ingredients and overseeing my little hands stir. I know the recipe by heart and even though my Grandma has long since passed, I continue to make chocolate chip cookies often. There is not a day where making cookies does not fit the bill—rainy days feel cozier with the warm smell of vanilla and chocolate wafting through the air; sunny days feel even brighter with a bite of cookie dough melting on my tongue; sad days feel happy, and happy days feel even happier. I am not looking to food as my comfort per say, but to the memories that accompany the baking (and tasting) process. As I measure and scoop, and crack the egg, I pause and reflect on the past, present, and future. I remember my Grandma: the sound of her voice, the touch of her hands, and I thank God for blessing me with her and for these sweet memories I have. I think how much I miss her, and how I wish she were still here. I also grab hold of God's promises and know that I will see her beautiful face in Heaven on some glorious future day.

I always need Jesus, but somedays I also need a spoonful of reminiscent cookie dough.

Jesus is my Rock, my Peace, my Hope, my Joy, my Salvation. He is my True Source of comfort and love. He is so good and kind—He puts people in His children's lives to be a source of comfort and love too.

Psalm 119:76, "May your unfailing love be my comfort, according to your promise to your servant."

Do you need Jesus and a bite of cookie dough today?

Thank God for sweet memories of loved ones who come to mind, and for the comfort He brings to your life.

Dear Lord,

Amen.

Delight

Bow your knee in surrender.

Lift your arms in worship.

Open your mouth in praise.

Walk in the way of righteousness.

Serve in the manner of humility.

Love the Lord whole-heartedly.

Love others unconditionally.

Look to the needs of others.

Live a life devoted to God.

Pursue His purpose and seek His plan in every area of your life.

Most importantly, enjoy your relationship with Jesus.

These are the things in which the Lord finds delight.

Funny thing—delighting the Lord also brings delight to our lives.

Psalm 149:4, "For the LORD takes delight in his people; He crowns the humble with victory."

How has living for the Lord brought delight to you?

Enter In

Lord, we, the people You created in Your very Own Image, come before You humble in heart, overcome with awe and wonder. As we enter Your Holy Presence our worries are appeased, our fears are calmed, our busy minds cease, our hearts are filled, and our bodies are stilled as Your Spirit washes over us. We enter Your Presence with our eyes open and our ears attuned, as we expectantly wait to hear what You have to say. In Your Presence we find peace that passes understanding, joy that exceeds our circumstances, and hope that helps us press on. We find love that holds us securely in Your Almighty grasp. In Your Presence blessings pour out and surround us. In Your Presence, all our needs are met, *beyond what we could ask for or imagine.*

As we enter Your Presence throughout our day, our lives are powerfully impacted, and our hearts forever changed.

As we enter Your holy and glorious Presence, we cannot help but be overcome and respond with gratitude, thanksgiving, and praise. Amen.

Psalm 21:6, "Surely you have granted him unending blessings and made him glad with the joy of your presence."

Pause right now and enter the Lord's Presence. Quiet your mind and focus on Him; be awed by His glory; be humbled by His holiness; be comforted by His love. Be refreshed and inspired; be overcome with gratitude. Be glad and rejoice; give thanks and worship.

Perfect

Lord, Your Law is perfect, and Your ways are just. Your holy standard remains the same throughout the ages; Your perfect measure of righteousness stands the test of time. Your commands for Your children are pure and lead us on the path of everlasting goodness.

At the end of time as we know it, when our Almighty Lord returns, those who placed their faith in Jesus and trusted Him as their Savior will receive their eternal reward. We will find our names have been written in Your *Book of Life* and read aloud for all to hear. We will stand before Your Throne with glory crowning our heads. The price and punishment for our sins has already been paid in full when Jesus gave His life on the Cross. We trust in Your perfect sacrificial love. We will be invited to take our place in Your Kingdom and live in the reality of our salvation forevermore. We will find comfort in the fact that we have been declared *not guilty*!

The judgment we will encounter as the children of God is not one of condemnation, but rather one that tests the enduring quality of our works—how did we invest our time, treasure, and talents with the life we were given on earth? Did we love others and show them mercy? Did we forgive trespasses committed against us and offer up grace? Did we share what we had with those in need? Did we encourage others with the Message of Jesus? Did we pass on God's blessing of peace? Did we share the hope that we have within us? Did we shine like the stars in the night sky and spread joy in the darkened world? Did we point others to the Savior with our testimony and actions? Did we live our lives according to the Word of God?

Lord, Your measure of perfection is bound by holy love; Your standard of justice is found in the Cross; Your guide to righteousness is found in Your unchanging Word.

When I stand before Your Throne someday, I hope to hear the words, *"Well done, My good and faithful servant,"* spoken of me. As I look back someday, I pray that my life on this planet was well-invested in Your Kingdom by sharing the Hope of the world. I pray to see that my life was used to spur others on toward faith in the Savior—that my life had eternal impact and value leading others to join me in the Family of God. I pray that my life accurately represented Your perfect love, mercy, and justice. Amen.

Matthew 25:21, "His master replied, 'Well done, good and faithful servant! You have been faithful with a few things; I will put you in charge of many things. Come and share your master's happiness!'"

How do these words from Matthew inspire you to live for God?

Cartwheels

Who says only kids get to have fun? The joy of the Lord makes it impossible for me to follow a mindset such as this. There are days when I am on a walk with the Lord and I can barely contain the joy deep inside; my heart skips a beat and my feet do as well. Despite aches and pains and the threat of new sprains, cartwheels call my name. My joy just abounds, running barefoot through tender green grass and the sprinkles of rain dancing on my skin sound enticingly delightful. I sing and I dance with silly abandon. The joy of the Lord takes over and renews my strength, and it keeps me young, even if only in my mind. The Holy Spirit takes over and revives my life. I hope never to outgrow fun or stop playfully exhibiting the joy of the Lord. Spending time with Jesus always leaves me with an uncontainable countenance of joy, and joy is quite contagious.

Psalm 89:15-16, "Blessed are those who have learned to acclaim you, who walk in the light of your presence, LORD. They rejoice in your name all day long; they celebrate your righteousness."

How does the joy of the Lord affect you?

Evidence

If I ever feel uncertain about God's goodness, I need only look back over the course of my life and there I will surely find evidence of His faithfulness, love, and grace dotted all throughout. There are endless proofs of His sheer goodness towards me, countless markers of His workings and provision, and innumerable testaments of His miraculous and merciful interventions. There is certifiable evidence to the goodness of God, of this I can personally testify. God's fingerprints are indelibly imprinted on my life, my heart, and my mind. He has continually pursued me and drawn my heart closer to His. He has guided me toward His ways of righteousness, and He has continued to redirect my feet back onto His path whenever I began to lose focus and wander away. He has blessed me beyond measure even when I didn't deserve it. He has loved me when I have been unlovable. He has shown me new mercies when I would have given up on myself. He has showered me with grace upon grace, calling me His new creation. He has protected me from evil and harm, under the shelter of His wings. He has lifted my spirits when they had fallen in despair. He has placed people throughout my life that have directed me to Him. He has opened gates and closed doors according to His sovereign knowledge and perfect will for me. These traces of God's Presence in my life reveal His immensely loving heart, His enduring faithfulness, His motives of pure goodness, and His vast capacity for mercy.

Psalm 23:6, "Surely your goodness and love will follow me all the days of my life, and I will dwell in the house of the LORD forever."

What evidence of God's Presence do you see throughout your life?

Requires

As humans we tend to complicate our relationship with God. We come up with all sorts of ways to approach Him and make a long list of obligations meant to please Him. Fortunately for us, God is in the business of simplifying things and calls us into a relationship with Himself purely through faith—faith in His amazing gift of grace extended to us through the sacrifice of Jesus. Our faith that God's grace is more than sufficient to cancel our debt and forgive our sins is all that is required for us to be made right with Him. Likewise, the Lord equally simplifies our life going forward. Two short phrases from Scripture clearly define the Lord's will for us. They reveal the kind of heart the Lord desires and demonstrate the sort of actions He requires. God does not place a heavy burden of rules and regulations on our shoulders. He merely asks us to walk humbly with Him and act justly toward others. He reminds us to rejoice, pray, and give thanks at all times because He knows it will make our hearts lighter. Our God is merciful, loving, and kind. The things He requires are for His glory and our own good! How do the Lord's requirements simplify life for you?

Micah 6:8, "He has shown you, O mortal, what is good. And what does the LORD require of you? To act justly and to love mercy and to walk humbly with your God."

1 Thessalonians 5:16-18, "Rejoice always, pray continually, give thanks in all circumstances; for this is God's will for you in Christ Jesus."

Extraordinary Faith

The Bible is filled with stories about regular people like you and me. So how did they merit a place of such honor as to be remembered and discussed all these thousands of years later? It was not by their own capabilities or power. Quite simply, they were ordinary folks with extraordinary faith. The names and faces that fill the pages of Scripture are those of shepherds, fishermen, tentmakers, seamstresses, fathers and mothers, husbands and wives, sons and daughters, boat-builders, and gardeners. They dealt with insecurities and struggled with sin. They were flawed and imperfect people, made perfect in the sight of God only by faith and His amazing grace. Despite their flaws and their failures, they believed God and everything He said to them. When they fell, they got right back up; when they veered off the path, they got back on track; when they lost their way, they refocused their sights on God. Just like you and me, they messed up from time to time. At times it even appears they took a step or two backwards in their walk with the Lord, but the overall trajectory of their lives was moving forward in faith, holding tightly to the hand of God. Extraordinary faith is what makes these folks so noteworthy. As we read the stories of those who have gone before us, let's find comfort in knowing we don't have to earn God's mercy or grace, we simply need to surrender our lives to Him in child-like faith.

Hebrews 11:1-2, "Now faith is confidence in what we hope for and assurance about what we do not see. This is what the ancients were commended for."

How does this encourage you in your walk of faith?

51

Faithful

Lord, You are good to Your core and Your promises are true. Your love for us is faithful and Your ways for us are just. You are an anchor for our souls when the waves of life seek to set us adrift and relentlessly toss us about. You alone keep our heads above water when the currents try to pull us under. You are the horizon that steadies our minds and the sun that warms our hearts. You are the One we cling to; Yours is the hope that carries us through. Help me to keep my eyes firmly fixed on You. Amen.

Psalm 145:13-14, "The LORD is faithful to all His promises and loving toward all He has made. The LORD upholds all those who fall and lifts up all who are bowed down."

Reflect on all the ways the Lord has been faithful to you. How does this affirm your faith in Him?

Falling Walls

When Joshua and the Israelites conquered the city of Jericho, it was not by force, but through worship. Under the Lord's direction, they circled the towering walls of the fortified city seven times. At the end of the seventh go-around, it was their loud shouts of praise that brought the walls crashing down, ushering in their victory. They obediently followed the Lord's lead, even when it didn't make sense. It was not their own strength, planning, or might, that gave them such triumph, it was their faith. They trusted the goodness and power of the Lord, knowing He would fulfill His promise. This story holds a valuable lesson for us: whatever battles we face, our best line of defense is to worship the Lord, seek His instruction, and follow through on what He says. In the face of obstacles, we must not lean on our understanding, but depend on Him by faith. The most vital components of winning our battles are praise, obedience, and faith. Let's trust God to see us through and accomplish victories in our lives.

Joshua 6:20, "When the trumpets sounded, the army shouted, and at the sound of the trumpet, when the men gave a loud shout, the wall collapsed; so everyone charged straight in, and they took the city."

How can praising the Lord give you peace in your battles? How has God given you victory in unexpected ways?

Far Better

The message of the Cross is oh, so sweet—Jesus died so that you and I could live in glory forever. I can think of no greater honor and privilege for us than to give up our lives for the sake of following Him in return. In surrendering our will, our goals, our purpose, our passions, and our plans we do not really lose anything of lasting value; we actually gain the greatest eternal treasure of all. Giving up our own agenda opens the door for the Lord to take control and move us in His direction. His ways exceed anything we can possibly conceive—they are far, far better! He calls us to follow Him and promises us eternal life with Him forever. Following Jesus whether by faith or by sight, is an enormous blessing in and of itself, but God goes above and beyond and even gives us a place of honor!

John 12:26, "Whoever serves me must follow me; and where I am, my servant also will be. My Father will honor the one who serves me.'"

Take a moment and thank Jesus for the blessing and privilege of following Him; thank Him for the promise of Heaven. Stand humbled at the fact that God will someday honor us in His Kingdom.

First Response

My goal is to look to the Lord as my first response, not as my last resort. It is much better and easier to ask for His direction, wisdom, and help at the onset of a situation, than to cry out in desperation for Him to fix what I have tried to do on my own. If I seek Jesus' guidance first, I can avoid making things into a bigger mess. He has the power and compassion to listen and help me no matter what point in my circumstance I ask, but it really simplifies everything if I pray and inquire first. This response does not always come easy—I'm more prone to impulsively react—but I am hopeful that the more I put it into practice the more naturally and instinctively I'll begin to seek God first.

Psalm 17:6, "I am praying to you because I know you will answer, O God. Bend down and listen as I pray."

Join me in prayer:

Lord, help me to seek You as my first response and not my last resort...

Amen.

Follow Me

Let's take up our cross and follow Jesus in an abundant life of humility, surrender, power, and victory. When we come to Him in faith, we find our salvation waiting. When we follow Him daily, we find direction for every step and mile of our journey. When we die to our sin and live in the reality of our new self that Christ has made us, life suddenly becomes surprisingly freeing. By following Jesus we discover true satisfaction; by intentionally living for Him, rather than aimlessly existing in this world we find our true purpose. Just as Jesus conquered death and stepped out of the grave, we follow in His footsteps and live as overcomers in the same manner. Jesus is the Way, and He shows us the path. Jesus calls us each by name and beckons us to follow closely alongside Him. The road He leads us on may veer in unexpected directions, but the destination ahead is the promise we cling to. He leads us every moment in our journey here on earth, but our hope of all hopes is that at the perfect time He will lead us homeward to His Heavenly Kingdom. Following Jesus is the best choice we can possibly make.

Starting here and now, each and every day, Jesus lovingly beckons us to take up our cross, to lay aside our own agendas, and follow Him wherever His takes us.

Matthew 16:24, "Then Jesus said to his disciples, "Whoever wants to be my disciple must deny themselves and take up their cross and follow me."

What do you need to lay aside today in order to follow Jesus today?

Freedom

The constraints of human-inspired religion are much like a corset tightly laced around our ribcage, squeezing the breath from our bodies, restricting the air to our lungs and our spirits, confining our ability to move carefree as the Lord intends.

Fortunately for us, the life, death, and resurrection of Jesus loosens the binds of religion and sets us free from its external constrictions. Jesus invites us to live and move in freedom through our relationship with Him. He redeems, restores, and revives us, bringing life to our weary bones, and in return we serve Him by being His hands and feet of mercy in this world. He breathes His very own breath into our lungs, and in turn we sing His praises. In our freedom we whole-heartedly love the Lord our God, and joyfully proclaim the Good News of the One who came to set the captives free. Jesus calls us to step out of the formality of religion and into a personal relationship with Him. He tells us to lay down our burdens and shed the heavy yoke of rules and regulations, and simply walk in unison with Him. He came to set us free from a life of perfectionism, works, and uncertainty, and gives us the blessed assurance of salvation and eternal security.

Thank You, Lord for the blessing of such a wonderful freedom of walking closely with You. Amen.

Galatians 5:1, "It is for freedom that Christ has set us free. Stand firm, then, and do not let yourselves be burdened again by a yoke of slavery."

How has Jesus set you free from perfectionism and religion?

Possibility

A new year. A new week. A new day. A new moment. An empty calendar. A blank page. A vacant box. A fresh possibility.

What if we embraced each of these things as occasions to pause before our sovereign Lord and ask Him for direction? Direction on the overall course of our lives, and for our minute-by-minute decisions?

What if we saw our time as the gift from God that it really is?

What if we genuinely appreciated each moment?

What if we recognized the new mercies and amazing grace our God pours out each morning?

What if we consciously seized the endless opportunities that God continually presents?

What if we used our time to draw near to God and pursue all that He has in store for us?

Imagine how blessed we would be. Let's celebrate the New Year, and commemorate each new week, and step into each new day, and face each brand-new moment by placing God first and seeking His ways.

Matthew 6:33, "But seek first his kingdom and his righteousness, and all these things will be given to you as well."

How does viewing time as a fresh possibility change your perspective on life?

Generous

Lord, as You are generous with me, help me to be generous with others—generous with my time, treasures, and talents. Help me to be generous with my words and actions, with my patience, kindness, love, mercy, and grace, with my attention, care, and thoughtfulness.

Help me to be extravagantly generous to the sacrificial extent of the generosity You have shown me. You generously gave Your Son Jesus as a sacrifice for me; You set me free from sin and death; You shower me in amazing grace and show me undeserved mercies which are new every day. You give me the hope of a generous inheritance, of eternity in Heaven with You. You flood my heart, mind, and soul with Your generous love; You meet all my earthly needs from Your Throne high above in the heavenly realm.

Lord, I fall to my knees overwhelmed by Your generosity towards me. Please help me to represent You well and live in the same generous manner.

Amen.

2 Corinthians 9:11, "You will be enriched in every way so that you can be generous on every occasion, and through us your generosity will result in thanksgiving to God."

What are some specific ways God has been generous with you? How can you live more generously?

Fulfillment

When we stand before the Lord someday, will we exclaim *"WOW!"* in amazed admiration, or stand silently in awesome adoration? I believe that God's glory will be so spectacular, beyond anything our finite minds can imagine, that it will be all we can do to stand as He takes our breath away. As His Presence brings us to our knees, with our faces postured towards the ground, we will impulsively respond in profound humility and worship. All that we had dreamed, all the promises we had clung to, all the hopes we had pressed on toward, will finally be revealed and experienced in full clarity and tangibility. What before was dim and clouded, what our minds could barely comprehend, will blaze brilliantly before us, as we come before the Throne gazing at our Lord in the fullness of His glory. This will be the moment when Heaven becomes our new reality. What was just out of reach before, will find complete fulfillment as Jesus stretches out His arms once more—this time with the purpose of embracing us and welcoming us Home.

Ephesians 1:9-10, "He made known to us the mystery of his will according to his good pleasure, which he purposed in Christ, to be put into effect when the times reach their fulfillment—to bring unity to all things in heaven and on earth under Christ."

How does the future fulfillment of God's Heavenly Promises spur you on each day?

Goodness

Heavenly Father, I pray that the people of this world, the members of my family, my friends both near and far, my neighbors and community would all notice and acknowledge the evidence of Your goodness that is all around. That instead of simply appreciating the goodness of Your beautiful creation, they would marvel at the goodness of their Creator; that the glowing sunset which takes their breath away, would remind them of the One who gives them life and breath; that the sun, moon, and stars which shine at night, would bring to their mind Your Son Jesus, our glorious Light. I pray that the feel of cool fresh water on their tongue would elicit a thirst for Your Living Water; that a delicious meal would give them a hunger for their Savior, the very Bread of Life. I pray that the warm embrace of a loved one would lead them to Your unconditional, everlasting, pure and holy love. I pray that all things, simple and spectacular, would lead people to find the goodness of Your Holy Presence.

I pray that all that is good in this world would serve as a powerful testimony to our hearts and minds as to Your all-surpassing goodness, and that in turn would give You praise. Amen.

Psalm 34:8, "Taste and see that the LORD is good; blessed is the one who takes refuge in him."

What testimonies of God's goodness do you witness in this world?

Future Generations

Reflecting on everything that I wish to see in our world makes me consider if I am doing my share to leave a positive mark. I realize that what society as a whole passes on to the next generation is of vital importance. But I must start with myself and consider if I am doing my part. I passionately desire for others to know Jesus. I want attitudes and acts of kindness, compassion, and service to be commonplace occurrences. I long for the world to be crowded with people whose hearts are grounded in humility and overflowing with kindness. I wish to see lives led by righteousness, mercy, and justice. I want to hear words expressing gratitude and grace—simple phrases like *please, thank you,* and *you're welcome, excuse me, no problem,* and *you go first.* I long for songs of praise and worship to God to be an expected and accepted part of everyday life. Am I doing my part in passing on such a beautiful and much-needed legacy?

The next generation cannot learn or live these things out unless they have been modeled and taught. I realize that unless I, along with the current generation consciously lead by example, these beliefs, attitudes, and behaviors could become a lost art. The future generations depend on us to pass along what is lovely, true, and good in the eyes of God.

Let's not drop the ball or become complacent in handing down our faith, values, morals, and manners. Let's be purposeful and diligent in guiding the future generations to seek and live in a way that pleases the Lord.

Deuteronomy 4:9-10, "Only be careful, and watch yourselves closely

so that you do not forget the things your eyes have seen or let them fade from your heart as long as you live. Teach them to your children and to their children after them. Remember the day you stood before the LORD your God at Horeb, when he said to me, 'Assemble the people before me to hear my words so that they may learn to revere me as long as they live in the land and may teach them to their children.'"

How do these verses personally encourage you to share your faith, morals, and values with the next generation?

Gingersnap

The other day my son and I were having a conversation about how people and situations can unexpectedly cause us to become snappy. Unfortunately, our first instinct in many confrontations or tribulations is to impulsively react without intent to hurt or without thought of repercussions, but much like the snapping turtle we chomp down and leave a nasty mark. Fortunately, there is another way for us to engage—one that is much more pleasing to God and a blessing for us and to others. We can thoughtfully pause and respond like a gingersnap—maintaining a touch of honest spice but conducting ourselves with gentleness, sincerity, and grace that leaves sweetness lingering in its place. Pondering the two vastly different mindsets—the snapping turtle and the gingersnap—and their varying implications, causes me to consider how my own moods, words, and actions leave a residual impression and have a lasting impact on everyone around.

I pray that God would help me to be more like the gingersnap and less like the snapping turtle. I pray that the Lord would help me thoughtfully respond instead of impulsively reacting to situations and people; that my existence in this world would represent Him well, leaving an impression of honesty, kindness, joy, truth, mercy, and love. I hope to overflow with the warm fragrance of Jesus and the taste of His grace wherever I venture, and with everyone I encounter. The more time I spend with the Lord, the better able and equipped I am to live like this. The more I am in His Presence, the more His Spirit flows through me. Does this example resonate with you?

Philippians 4:5, "Let your gentleness be evident to all. The Lord is near."

Gracious Act

(Kindly remember the following was written during a year-long quarantine at home due to a worldwide pandemic.)

What if rather than seeing our current world events as evidence of God's anger being poured out on us, or even worse, as a sign of His disinterest in our lives, we saw them as gracious acts meant to grab our attention and draw our hearts back to Him? What if we viewed this as an opportunity to put Him back on the throne of our lives and reprioritize everything accordingly? Maybe, just maybe, God is giving us and our land this extended Sabbath rest so that we can once again appreciate the simple blessings in life—things like watching sunsets, riding bikes, taking walks, flying kites, playing games, having heartfelt conversations, opening our Bibles, and spending precious time talking with Him. What if God has brought things to a standstill just so we can be still and stand in His Presence. Knowing His merciful character, this could very well be His compassionate and gracious act.

Psalm 145:7-9, "They celebrate your abundant goodness and joyfully sing of your righteousness. The LORD is gracious and compassionate, slow to anger and rich in love. The LORD is good to all; he has compassion on all he has made."

Name a blessing you experience during God-ordained rest.

Party Clothes

If Jesus came to give us abundant life, why are there still days when we walk around feeling numbly dead on the inside, appearing to be in mourning on the outside? I believe it is because we are forgetful of the fact that we have been set free from the curse of sin, and that we have been called out of the grave into new life and freedom. In light of our newness of life, we should be filled with hope, tearing off our old grave clothes, replacing them with *a garment of praise* (Isaiah 61:3). Reflecting on what the Lord has done for us should change our somber outlook into a countenance of grateful celebration. The unpleasant stench of death should no longer surround us, rather the sweet aroma of joy should be our new fragrance. We once were dead in our sins, but now we have been made alive in Christ. Jesus has rolled the stone away and has called us out of the dark; I think it is time we put on our party clothes and dress the part!

John 11:43-44, "When he had said this, Jesus called in a loud voice, 'Lazarus, come out!' The dead man came out, his hands and feet wrapped with strips of linen, and a cloth around his face. Jesus said to them, 'Take off the grave clothes and let him go.'"

Have you taken off your grave clothes and put on your new life in Christ? Are you living in the reality of your liberation?

Unity

Unity—a concept that is greatly desired in this world, but also seemingly elusive when approached through our human effort. This past year has brought the concept and craving for *unity* to the forefront of our streets, our news, our hearts, and our lives. I enjoy doing research, so I thought I would check to see how much *unity* is currently on our minds. I looked at two popular social media platforms and discovered that one has 2.5 million hashtags for the word *unity* and the other has a whopping 7 million. Apparently, the quest for *unity* is on the rise.

I also took a minute to look up the definition of *unity*.

Here is what I found: the quality or state of not being multiple; oneness; a condition of harmony; accord; continuity without deviation or change (as in purpose or action); the quality or state of being made one; unification

Unity is not something that can be forced or manufactured by society. The unity we long for and strive for is only truly possible by the love and power of God working in us and among us. The oneness, the harmony and accord, being one in purpose and action—these sound a lot like what the Lord offers to us in His family. God is the One who bridges all our gaps; He tears down walls and builds bridges for us to cross over. Everything that divides us falls away when we acknowledge God as our Creator and recognize that He is the one who breathes life into every single human being on this planet. Each of us has priceless value and worth in His eyes. We are all made in His image and called to reflect His glory.

God is extremely creative—just take a walk outside in nature and witness the diversity in all His creation. He didn't make the flowers all one color and one scent; the trees vary in their shades of green; the sky reflects a wide spectrum of colors. Though it is not all exactly the same, all of nature proclaims His glory. God did not make all people identical either—that would have been boring. He created a new mold and special details in each one of us. God has given each of us unique features, distinct personalities, different likes and dislikes, talents, skills, gifts, backgrounds, languages, cultures, life experiences, and varying shades of pink, tan, and brown. It becomes obvious as we look at our world today, that these beautiful differences can cause misunderstandings, fear, and harmful assumptions among us. When we look to God and allow Him to change our perspective of ourselves and each other, that's when unity can become a reality.

Being in women's ministry has put me in the position to see this unity come to life. I have met women from various backgrounds, ethnicities, and of a wide range of ages, and I consider them my dearest friends. The most wonderful thing happens when we come together—all our differences fade away and our love for Jesus becomes our great uniter. We see each other as sisters-in-Christ who have the <u>same</u> Heavenly Father; we are all redeemed sinners who have the <u>same</u> Savior; we have the <u>same</u> Holy Spirit dwelling inside us; we have the <u>same</u> faith in Jesus that spurs us on; we have the <u>same</u> hope of Heaven that calls us home. God's greatest desire is that everyone would receive His Son Jesus as their own personal Savior, join His family, and enjoy unity as He designed it.

Jesus intends for His church to represent Him well by showing what unity can look like—we are meant to love each other in His Name. True unity is wrapped up in the gift and Gospel of Jesus. We get to be the ones who deliver it and pray that others would receive it! Unity is possible with Jesus!

Ephesians 4:1-6, "I urge you to live a life worthy of the calling you have received. Be completely humble and gentle; be patient, bearing with one another in love. Make every effort to keep the unity of the Spirit through the bond of peace. There is one body and one Spirit, just as you were called to one hope when you were called; one Lord, one faith, one baptism; one God and Father of all, who is over all and through all and in all."

How have you experienced unity in the family of God? How can you help spread the unity God desires with the world?

Beyond Measure

Our God is infinite. He is limitless and without bounds. He is immeasurable, and yet by Him everything and everyone finds their measure. He is incomprehensible, far beyond our finite understanding. Our earthbound vision offers us only a glimpse of His glory; our limited human minds grasp only a partial knowledge of God's eternal being. Someday though when we see Him face-to-face, we will finally perceive Him more clearly. When we step into eternity and the veil of our sin is removed, then unobscured we will behold the brilliance of His majesty.

God alone is self-existent, the Great I AM—He is the Alpha and Omega, the beginning and the end. He is reliant on no one, but all are reliant on Him. God needs no one, but we draw our every breath from Him. Even though our understanding of God is limited, we gain a great knowledge of our identity in relation to Him. He is our mighty King; He is our sovereign Lord; He is our blessed Savior; He is our omnipotent Creator. We are His beloved children—chosen and adopted, saved and redeemed, forgiven and made new in Christ.

God is the only One who makes something out of nothing. His power and authority are without bounds. He pursues broken hearts and with His love He makes them whole. He redeems shattered lives and rebuilds them with promises of hope and a future. He restores the weary and downtrodden and makes their spirits soar on wings like eagles. He pours into empty vessels and makes them overflow with the goodness of the Lord. He meets the lost and lonely and guides them to seek refuge under the shelter of His wings.

God Himself is beyond measure; our identity is measured by our relationship with Him. The blessings He pours out on us are more than we can count, ask, or imagine.

Isaiah 40:12-13, "Who has measured the waters in the hollow of his hand, or with the breadth of his hand marked off the heavens? Who has held the dust of the earth in a basket, or weighed the mountains on the scales and the hills in a balance? Who can fathom the Spirit of the LORD, or instruct the LORD as his counselor?"

How do these truths about the nature of God bring blessed assurance to your heart?

Healing

Our world is filled with people whose hearts are broken and spirits are wounded. Try as we might, all the glue in our cupboards and all bandages in the world will never suffice in healing us or binding us back together. Only the love and power of God can do that. Healing is not found by willing it up from within ourselves, or by persevering in our own strength; healing is found outside our bounds, in the limitless grace and compassion of God. He formed the universe and everything in it, by merely speaking it into existence. The sound of His voice creates new things—where there is hopelessness, He speaks hope; where there is sorrow, He speaks comfort; where there is despair, He speaks joy; where there is chaos, He speaks peace; where there is division, He speaks unity; where there is darkness, He speaks light; where there is death, He speaks life. He who holds the stars in their place can do all of this and more. He is the Lord God Almighty, and power and healing are found in His Name.

Psalm 147:3-5, "He heals the brokenhearted and binds up their wounds. He determines the number of the stars and calls them each by name. Great is our Lord and mighty in power; his understanding has no limit."

Where do you need the Lord's healing today?

Home at Last

Home. What a beautiful word! It represents a place where we belong and matter; a place where we retreat to find safety and security; a place where warmth envelops us, and love abounds. Jesus is preparing such a home with us specifically in mind. It will be a refuge where we find perfect peace and our restless souls will settle in and find their rest. In this future heavenly dwelling we literally abide with Jesus. Our hearts will discover lasting contentment in His Presence. No longer will we run to and fro, seeking a place to call our own. Jesus has a permanent residence set aside with your name and my name written on it. It will be a place like none we have ever experienced before! When Jesus comes back, He will take us to be with Him—that is His promise to us, and His promises are always true.

John 14:1-4, ""Do not let your hearts be troubled. You believe in God; believe also in me. My Father's house has many rooms; if that were not so, would I have told you that I am going there to prepare a place for you? And if I go and prepare a place for you, I will come back and take you to be with me that you also may be where I am. You know the way to the place where I am going."

How does the promise of this heavenly Home comfort you in the moment and fill you with hope for the future?

Honeycomb

You have most likely heard the phrase, *"put your foot in your mouth,"* and maybe you have even experienced this unpleasant event in your own life. It is when you have said something you shouldn't have, and you wish you could take it back. Feet usually spend hours in hot sweaty socks and shoes, and they do not sound all that appetizing. We definitely want to avoid doing that.

Another phrase that gives us caution about our words reminds us that, *"we may have to eat our words."* I don't know about you, but I'd prefer to eat sweet words rather than bitter ones. I want my words to taste pleasant on my tongue and leave no sour aftertaste.

We have a lot less regret when we think about what we are going to say before we let it pop out of our mouths. I have a friend who carefully considers every word before she speaks it. I admire her so much! Her words are kind and encouraging even when she is giving some correction. The vast amount of time she spends in prayer helps train her up in being quick to listen. She holds her tongue until you are finished speaking and then thoughtfully responds. I don't think she's ever interrupted or rushed me. As she listens to every one of your words, you realize that she is praying even as you speak. The words that come out of her mouth are always a blessing, because as she listens to you, she is also listening for the Lord's wisdom. She is the perfect example of *quick to listen, slow to speak, and slow to anger.* I honestly do not remember ever seeing her angry.

Do you know a friend like this? Can the same be said of you?

Proverbs 16:24, "Gracious words are a honeycomb, sweet to the soul and healing to the bones."

Here is another cautionary verse for us to consider:

Ecclesiastes 5:2, "Do not be quick with your mouth, do not be hasty in your heart to utter anything before God. God is in heaven and you are on earth, so let your words be few."

How can taking a pause before speaking help you avoid regret?

Certainty

Seasons come and seasons go; seeds take root and blooms fade. All things of this earth have a beginning and an end; everything has a birth and also a death. The only certainty we have on this planet is the unchanging character of God. He does not shift like shadows cast on the pavement which are subject to the sun's placement in the heavens throughout the day. He is the Lord of Heaven; His glory forever remains the same. The waves and currents may etch away at the shoreline of our lives, but they will never cause the Lord to crumble. He is the Rock of Ages, the firm foundation beneath our feet. Because God is unchanging in His essence and nature, we can completely depend on the certainty of His faithfulness, His love, His mercy, His grace, His power, His strength! All fear, worry, and anxiety are removed when we place our faith and hope in Him. With our eyes fixed on Jesus, uncertainty becomes a thing of the past.

He alone is our blessed assurance!

James 1:17, "Every good and perfect gift is from above, coming down from the Father of the heavenly lights, who does not change like shifting shadows."

How does the unchanging character of God inspire confidence in you?

If Only

People are clamoring above one another to have their voices heard. Individuals assert that what they have to say is most important, and that they hold the answer to the world's problems in their hands. What society really needs is to be still before the Lord, listen to our Heavenly Father, and seek His ways as we reside on the earth. Our desire should be for the words of Jesus to be heard throughout the world—His words of truth, love, hope, healing, joy, and justice to be ringing through the streets and playing continually in our ears. Everyone is striving and pushing their own selfish agenda when what we truly need are the selfless plans of God to lead us forward. If everyone would just be stilled and quieted for even a moment, then maybe His voice could be heard. The world is so loud with anger and hatred, panic and fear—only God can break through the madness, quiet our hearts, and bring the lasting peace we so earnestly desire. If only we would seek Him, then He would heal our hearts, our homes, and our land.

Let us seek Him together today!

2 Chronicles 7:13-15, ""When I shut up the heavens so that there is no rain, or command locusts to devour the land or send a plague among my people, if my people, who are called by my name, will humble themselves and pray and seek my face and turn from their wicked ways, then I will hear from heaven, and I will forgive their sin and will heal their land. Now my eyes will be open and my ears attentive to the prayers offered in this place."

Longing

I believe that God allows difficult circumstances to shake up our lives for the good purpose of loosening our grip on this uncertain world; He also allows trials into our lives as reminders to tighten our grasp on Him and the certainties that His Kingdom brings. The disease that we face makes us long for glorified bodies; the violence and hatred that is prevalent among us makes us long for His love and justice to rule from the heavenly places; the division and selfishness that separates people makes us long for the unity that only Christ can bring. The more chaotic this world becomes, the more intensely I long for Jesus, and He is always faithful to fulfill that longing in my heart. Someday all of my longings will be fully realized when I enter Heaven's Gates.

2 Corinthians 5:2-4, "Meanwhile we groan, longing to be clothed instead with our heavenly dwelling, because when we are clothed, we will not be found naked. For while we are in this tent [these earthly bodies], we groan and are burdened, because we do not wish to be unclothed but to be clothed instead with our heavenly dwelling, so that what is mortal may be swallowed up by life."

How do you personally feel this longing ache within your own body and soul?

In the Midst

Though the world seems to spin out of control, God remains the same. He is our constant source of stability and strength. He is where our hope lies. In the midst of darkness, He is our Light. In the midst of confusion, He is our clarity. In the midst of chaos, He is our calm. In the midst of lies, He is our truth. In the midst of hate, He is our love. In the midst of sin, He is our Savior. In the midst of death, He is our life. In the midst of our questions, He is our answer. In the midst of change, He remains unshakable.

Our Lord and Savior, Creator and Maker remains the same every single day—today, tomorrow, and forever.

Hebrews 13:8, "Jesus Christ is the same yesterday and today and forever."

What circumstance are *you* currently in the midst of that you need to feel the stable Presence of God?

Abide

Lord, help me to not depart from You or Your ways; to not wander from Your will or the path You lay out for me; to not drift from Your Presence or leave the protective shadow of Your wings. I confess that on my own I grow weak and weary; I fall and struggle to get back up; I am forgetful of Your goodness and go off in my own direction. When I attempt to do things in my own strength and effort, I find that all those endeavors are only in vain. Without Your blessing upon me and Your sovereign Hand to guide me, all my pursuits and energies are fruitless and leave me feeling empty inside. Far too often I have spoken or acted without first inquiring of You, and each of those times I have noticed that my words fall flat, and my deeds are unsatisfying. You alone anoint me and supply all my needs. Help me to constantly abide in You. May I always give pause throughout my day, to seek You first in all things. May I rest in the blessed shelter of Your protection and find inspiration in the truth of Your words. I pray to be filled with Your Holy Spirit and to have Your Holy Word stored up in me. I desire to spend time with You daily; to sit at Your feet, be overcome in adoration, to listen and hear what You would say. I ask to be filled in Your Presence to the point of overflowing, so that whatever comes out of my mouth or is done by my hands is inspired by You.

Thank you, Lord for inviting me to abide in You! Amen.

John 15:4, "Remain in me, as I also remain in you. No branch can bear fruit by itself; it must remain in the vine. Neither can you bear fruit unless you remain in me."

Invaluable Gift

Recently a friend sent me a message saying I had been on her mind, and she had been praying for me. For reasons yet unknown to me, God placed me in her thoughts prompting her to intercede on my behalf. I am extremely grateful for a friend who heeds the call of God and loves me in this way. As I told my friend, prayers are an invaluable gift both to give and receive; they are the act of inviting God's blessing, power, love, and Presence into our lives. Often, we ask permission to pray for one another—just so you know, there is no need to ask me. That is a question to which my reply is always, *"yes, please"* and *"thank you."* Prayers are always welcome and greatly appreciated.

1 Timothy 2:1, *"I urge, then, first of all, that petitions, prayers, intercession and thanksgiving be made for all people—"*

How readily do you ask others to pray for you? I encourage you to grab hold of this invaluable gift.

Incomparable

The most beautiful hand-sketched portrait, even if it's museum worthy, will never encapsulate all the finest details of you! The sparkle in your eyes and the laugh behind your smile can only be fully appreciated through a personal encounter with you. The complexity of *you* can only be fully appreciated through a face-to-face engagement—the captivating life within you to be truly revealed. Your beauty was sketched in fine detail by the pencil of the masterful Artist.

A landscape photo could never fully capture or compare to the magnificence of the real thing. The verdant pigment of the rolling hills and the breath-taking blue of the cerulean sky cannot be confined to a picture, a painting, or a screen. Although a photograph may be amazing and can evoke a sense of pleasure, to get the full impact we need to behold God's creation unfiltered with our very own eyes. Witnessing the real object as made by the hand of our Creator, evokes an overwhelming sense of awe and wonder.

The most exquisite watercolor of the seashore could never live up to the experience of feeling the salty breeze brushing past our face, or the sandy grains squishing underneath our feet. The sound of squawking seagulls, the highly-hoped-for dolphin sighting, and the joy of watching them playfully ride the waves, definitely need to be a first-hand experience. No swish of the brush could ever fully depict all of this. The exquisite artistry of our Lord is utterly unsurpassable.

The finest perfumes in all the world, even those from the most exclusive shops in Paris, pale in comparison to the fragrance of a God-grown, fresh-cut bouquet of roses or the sweet aroma of orange blossoms in spring drifting through the air. A trellis wrapped in night-blooming jasmine has an intoxicating way of filling the atmosphere. The luxurious scents of blooms grown from the earth have a way of both warming a heart and refreshing a soul. They impact our senses in a way that a manufactured fragrance cannot fully do. There is nothing quite like inhaling the perfumes made by the chemistry of God.

In the same way, the idols fashioned by the minds and hands of humans are nothing in the light of God's glory. They may look sparkly and alluring, but they cannot save us, help us, guide us, or comfort us in our time of need—they are useless when it comes right down to it, considering eternity. The temporary pleasures of this world will never fill our lives as abundantly as our eternal blessings—like hope, joy, and peace—coming from the Lord. I don't know about you, but I have no use for an idol, when I can have the real thing. The God I seek and the God I serve has the power and love to bountifully meet all my needs. There is no salvation like that from our Heavenly Father.

Though we try to recreate the Lord's marvelous creations, and as captivating as our attempts may be, they will never surpass His incomparable masterpieces. Everything the Lord touches reveals a glimpse of His splendid majesty. Jesus Himself is incomparable in every single way. Since I am given the choice, I choose Jesus— I choose to have the Real Thing.

Isaiah 40:26, "Look up into the heavens. Who created all the stars?

He brings them out like an army, one after another, calling each by

its name. Because of his great power and incomparable strength,

not a single one is missing."

How does the Lord's dazzling creativity put things in perspective and inspire you to worship Him?

Invited

It seems that almost daily I am receiving prayer requests from family and friends—prayers for healing, for provision, for direction, for protection, for peace, and restored hope. What a blessing to be a partner in prayer and an intercessor on behalf of loved ones—delivering their cares, requests, thanksgiving, and praises alongside my own to the throne room of God. Prayer is a blessing and opportunity that is far too often overlooked. Power, peace, hope, and even joy infuse our lives and situation any time we seize this invitation to intimately converse with God. Prayer is an occasion in which we bring our concerns to Him and lay them at His Sovereign feet. Prayer is the lifeline for you and me, connecting us with the Giver of Life Himself.

Let's take the opportunity to push pause on the busyness of life for a moment and step into the presence of God. Let's lay our burdens down and hear His calming Voice. Let's pray for one another and help carry each other's heavy loads, delivering them to the hands of God. We are invited to pray about anything and everything—nothing is too big or too small. We are invited to rest in the arms of the Father. Let's take advantage of this blessed invitation and pray without ceasing.

Ephesians 6:18, "And pray in the Spirit on all occasions with all kinds of prayers and requests. With this in mind, be alert and always keep on praying for all the Lord's people."

Ask God to increase your prayer life and grow your relationship with Him through these conversations.

Always and Never

Using the words *always* and *never*, Scripture gives us a clear picture of God's character and a firm foundation on which to stake our faith. There are many things God *always* does, and many things He will *never* do. These words describe the essence of His being and offer us profound hope in His consistency and in His faithful promises to us. Read the following verses to hear these truths for yourself.

Psalm 40:11, "Do not withhold your mercy from me, LORD; may your love and faithfulness **always** protect me."

Psalm 119:132, "Turn to me and have mercy on me, as you **always** do to those who love your name.

Psalm 119:144, "Your statutes are **always** righteous; give me understanding that I may live."

Isaiah 58:11, "The LORD will guide you **always**; he will satisfy your needs in a sun-scorched land and will strengthen your frame. You will be like a well-watered garden, like a spring whose waters never fail."

Keep reading, there are more to come...

Jeremiah 12:1, "You are **always** righteous, LORD, when I bring a case before you."

Matthew 28:20, "And surely I am with you **always**, to the very end of the age."

John 5:17, "In his defense Jesus said to them, "My Father is **always** at his work to this very day, and I too am working.""

2 Corinthians 2:14, "But thanks be to God, who **always** leads us as captives in Christ's triumphal procession and uses us to spread the aroma of the knowledge of him everywhere."

1 Corinthians 13:6-7, "[God's] Love does not delight in evil but rejoices with the truth. It **always** protects, **always** trusts, **always** hopes, **always** perseveres. [God's] Love **never** fails."

Genesis 9:11, "I establish my covenant with you: **Never** again will all life be destroyed by the waters of a flood; **never** again will there be a flood to destroy the earth."

Still a few more pages of hope for us....

Judges 2:1, "I brought you up out of Egypt and led you into the land I swore to give to your ancestors. I said, 'I will **never** break my covenant with you,'"

Deuteronomy 31:6, 8, "Be strong and courageous. Do not be afraid or terrified because of them, for the LORD your God goes with you; he will **never** leave you nor forsake you... Do not be afraid; do not be discouraged."

Psalm 9:18, "But God will **never** forget the needy; the hope of the afflicted will **never** perish."

Psalm 89:28, "I will maintain my love to him forever, and my covenant with him will **never** fail."

Psalm 94:14, "For the LORD will not reject his people; he will **never** forsake his inheritance." (We are His inheritance.)

Lamentations 3:22, "Because of the LORD's great love we are not consumed, for his compassions **never** fail."

Matthew 24:35, "Heaven and earth will pass away, but my words will **never** pass away."

Luke 1:32-34, "He will be great and will be called the Son of the Most High. The Lord God will give him the throne of his father David, and he will reign over Jacob's descendants forever; his kingdom will **never** end."

John 6:35, "Then Jesus declared, "I am the bread of life. Whoever comes to me will **never** go hungry, and whoever believes in me will **never** be thirsty."

John 6:37, "All those the Father gives me will come to me, and whoever comes to me I will **never** drive away."

John 8:12, "When Jesus spoke again to the people, he said, "I am the light of the world. Whoever follows me will **never** walk in darkness, but will have the light of life."

John 8:51, "Very truly I tell you, whoever obeys my word will **never** see death."

John 10:28, "I give them eternal life, and they shall **never** perish; no one will snatch them out of my hand."

One more page of promises...

1 Peter 1:3-5, "Praise be to the God and Father of our Lord Jesus Christ! In his great mercy he has given us new birth into a living hope through the resurrection of Jesus Christ from the dead, and into an inheritance that can **never** perish, spoil or fade. This inheritance is kept in heaven for you, who through faith are shielded by God's power until the coming of the salvation that is ready to be revealed in the last time."

Revelation 3:5, "The one who is victorious will, like them, be dressed in white. I will **never** blot out the name of that person from the book of life, but will acknowledge that name before my Father and his angels."

How do these *always* and *nevers* encourage you today? Is there a particular verse you especially needed to hear?

Tuck these promises into your heart and carry them with you wherever you go and for whatever you face.

Knowing

Knowing that God's love towards me steadfastly endures forever enables me to steadfastly endure difficult moments, days, and seasons. Knowing that He will never leave me or forsake me is a comfort for my soul and the boost of strength and courage that I need. Believing that His love for me cannot be shaken, diminished, or taken away helps my confidence in Him and in my identity as His child to remain unshaken as well. Knowing that His love for me is not fleeting, but will follow all the days of my life and rest on me throughout eternity, comforts my heart and lightens the burdens of my soul. I know without a doubt that Heaven is my God-ordained destiny, and I trust with all my heart that the Lord walks with me in Spirit daily here on earth. Someday I will encounter the Lord face-to-face, and the love and glory of His Presence will prove and affirm everything that I believe to be true of Him.

Psalm 9:10, "Those who know your name trust in you, for you, LORD,

have never forsaken those who seek you."

God's love for me endures forever—and that is a really long time. Just knowing this helps me confidently persevere until the glorious Day that I gaze directly into His beautiful Face.

How does this knowledge affect you?

Lead me

Lately it seems that the world is drowning in tragedy; we are knee-deep and neck-high in problems. Just turn on the T.V. to hear more bad news—worldwide virus, racism, hate, division, looting, riots, hurricanes, tornados, fires, etc. Besides the broad scope of issues, I have been hearing of much more personal struggles that hit closer to home—things such as illness, hospitalizations, job losses, and even death. I will stop there before I really get you down. I promise that's it for the doom and gloom, we will move onto the brighter side of things. Despite these tribulations we have a mighty hope. God is still in control; He is good; He is strong; He is extremely capable.

He gives my feet a firm and solid place to stand when it feels as if all the earth is fraught with sinking sand. He reaches out His hand, grabs hold of mine and pulls me up to safety, out of the reach of everything that tries so hard to drag me down. He leads me to a place that is higher than myself; higher than my struggles, my sadness, my despair; above the uncertainties and anxieties, to the Rock that is firm and secure. He leads me to a place where hope, faith, peace, and joy continually exist, even though hardships persist. He leads me to the calming refuge of His ever-loving Presence.

Psalm 61:1-2, "Hear my cry, O God; listen to my prayer. From the ends of the earth I call to you, I call as my heart grows faint; lead me to the rock that is higher than I."

Have you allowed God to lead you to the Rock that is higher than you or your circumstances?

Extravagant

Lord, help me to love with Your kind of love. Help me to love generously and graciously, overlooking faults and flaws, overcoming grudges and hurts. Help me to love sincerely from the bottom of my heart, with pure motives and goodness towards those in my circle and sphere. Help me to love fearlessly with no apprehension, offering comfort without reservations. Help me to love humbly, putting aside all pride and indignation. Put it on my heart to care for the needs of others and be eager to come alongside. Help me to love with the same dedication and resolve that You showed on the Cross; You stopped at nothing and even lay down Your life for my sake. Help me to love like You love Jesus—unconditionally, faithfully, and extravagantly. Help me to love in Your sacrificial way and in Your mighty Name.

1 John 4:9, *"This is how God showed his love among us: He sent his one and only Son into the world that we might live through him."*

How have you experienced God's extravagant love? Who is God asking you to extravagantly love in His Name?

Let Go and Hold On

You are safe within the arms of the Savior.

Open your heart.

Hand over your plans.

Surrender all your control.

Give the Lord everything you cling so tightly to—your hopes and dreams, your fears and anxieties, your passions and purpose, your safety and security.

Release everything you have to Him and trust that it is all in Good Hands.

Let go of everything, but by all means, dear beloved,

hold onto your glorious hope.

Psalm 71:14, "As for me, I will always have hope;

I will praise you more and more."

What do you need to let go of? What do you need to hold on to hope for?

Listen and Do

I have invested the better part of the last twenty years of my life in studying the Bible. If I had not let it change my life, it would have been a complete waste of my time. The reason we attend church, and the whole reason we study the Bible, is not to be entertained on a Sunday morning or to gain more head knowledge— it is so we can know the Lord and His Word better, and so it can impact our day-to-day life. When we open our Bibles, or listen to a sermon, or sit down to an in-depth study of the Word, it is with the intention of being transformed, more and more into the likeness of Jesus. Jesus' death on the Cross was the sacrifice that makes us right with God. No amount of good works can attain righteousness for us, only Jesus can do that. Once we place our faith in Jesus, our sins are no longer counted against us. Our slates are wiped clean and when God looks at us, He no longer sees our sins—He sees the righteousness of Christ. Because of Jesus we are made brand-new and the Spirit-filled us is here to stay. Having been made new, we now want to live accordingly, pursuing all that Jesus has in store for us. God's Word is the perfect guide for living a Christ-centered life. His Word is truly a blessing to read, but it is even more of a blessing to live out.

Is there an area where the Lord is convicting you to *listen and do*—to live out His Word more fully?

James 1:22-25 exhorts us to "not merely listen to the Word, and so deceive ourselves. We must do what it says."

Matthew 7:24, "Therefore everyone who puts these words of mine into practice is like a wise man who built his house on the rock."

Manifest

Jesus is the exact representation of our Heavenly Father. He is the precise embodiment of God's holy perfection; His sacrificial love and His unending mercy; His absolute justice and His amazing grace; His eternal wisdom and His absolute power. All these attributes were lived out in Jesus. Through His life God's divine existence was manifest and given flesh. To see Jesus is to glimpse God's glory. To know Jesus is to experience God's love. To hear the tender voice of Jesus is to hear the very heart of God. To walk with Jesus is to hold the hand of our Heavenly Father. To talk with Jesus is to enter the very Throne Room of God.

If we ever wonder what God is like we need only open His holy Word—He is revealed on every page. To better know the Father, we need only see how Jesus lived, hear the words He spoke, witness the love He shared, and feel the power He unleashed as He healed the broken of this earth.

We need only say *YES* to Jesus, and God will be made manifest in our hearts and our lives.

Hebrews 1:3, "The Son is the radiance of God's glory and the exact representation of his being, sustaining all things by his powerful word. After he had provided purification for sins, he sat down at the right hand of the Majesty in heaven."

How has the Lord's Presence been made manifest in your life?

Things Above

Colossians 3:1-4, "Since, then, you have been raised with Christ, set your hearts on things above, where Christ is, seated at the right hand of God. Set your minds on things above, not on earthly things. For you died, and your life is now hidden with Christ in God. When Christ, who is your life, appears, then you also will appear with him in glory."

These four verses hold significant insight into who Christ is, who I am in relation to Him, and how that knowledge should affect my life. These verses encourage me to *"set my heart and mind on things above"*—to keep a heavenly perspective, to hold onto my eternal hope, and to live my life in light of my relationship with Jesus. These verses remind me that Christ has been raised from the dead to glory and that He is now sovereignly seated in the heavenly realms at the right hand of God. They remind me that I have been raised with Christ and that my life is hidden and wrapped up in Him; they offer me the assured hope that my faithful Lord is coming back for me someday. These verses exhort me to focus my heart and mind on heavenly things, not the things of this world that often press in and surround me. These Scriptures kindle my confidence and help me push onward as I remember my future reward—I am promised I will be with my Savior in glory.

How do these verses encourage you to press on and persevere?

More of You

The infinite expanse of the heavens and the unplumbed depths of the sea declare the vastness of Your glory, which is incomprehensible to me. Standing under the canopy of stars You created, I feel incredibly small. Seated at the edge of the seashore I gaze out at the endless horizon pondering Your majesty and beauty, considering how You are the Creator of it all. My mind barely grasps the edges of the knowledge of Your greatness; my spirit scarcely catches the supernatural revelation of Your all-surpassing power. But from what I do know of You and what I have felt of Your Presence, I can say that I want more. To taste and glimpse Your glory leaves me to hunger and thirst for more of You. I long for more of Your love, Your peace, Your hope, Your joy. I long for your righteousness to dwell on this earth and be lived out in me. I long for Your Heavenly Kingdom to fill the earth. I long to see You face-to-face, Your glory unobscured. I long for more of You, my Savior and Lord.

Psalm 61:4, "I long to dwell in your tent forever and take refuge in the shelter of your wings."

How does your glimpse of God's glory evoke your desire for more of Him?

Marvel

This too shall pass is a phrase we use to bring comfort to ourselves and others who are wishing to skip ahead of difficult times. These words hold much more meaning than that though. This statement reminds us that both good and bad times pass quickly by. And if we are not careful, time will slip through our fingers without our even noticing. Busyness is a distractor; pain makes us long for time to go faster; boredom makes us lust for something other.

God wants to use all our days for our good and His glory; there are lessons to be gained through every situation. With God nothing is ever wasted. Instead of rushing through life and hastily pushing past, let us pause and reflect on the precious gift of time.

Let us lift our heads from our phones and computers to notice the people right around us.

Let us greet each other with a sincere welcome and a warm hug, relishing our moments together.

Let us do more than hear the words that someone is speaking; let us enter the moment and truly listen to what they are saying.

Let us get out of our comfort zones and into the great outdoors. Let us explore this amazing planet that the Lord has created.

Let us feel the grainy sand between our toes, the damp grass beneath our feet, the cool breeze on our cheeks, to gaze upon the wondrous beauty before our eyes. Let us stand in awe of God's creation and give Him worship and praise.

Let us come before God's throne and ask Him what He wants to teach us; what He wants us to tuck in our hearts and take with us as we journey along. Each moment is a priceless treasure not meant to be squandered, but thoroughly appreciated and grasped.

Our season on earth is fleeting, so let us stand fully in the moment aware of God's awesome presence and be grateful for the gift of time.

Let us be wholly present and marvel at our surroundings.

Ecclesiastes 3:11, "He has made everything beautiful in its time. He has also set eternity in the human heart; yet no one can fathom what God has done from beginning to end."

What about this day has caused you to marvel? If nothing comes to you yet, I suggest slowing down, quieting your mind, and lifting your eyes.

Morning Glory

This morning I slipped into my chair to seize a moment of quiet solitude with the Lord. From my vantage point I soaked in the great outdoors and observed the stillness of the atmosphere.

I noticed a coolness lingered weightlessly in the air.

The cobwebs glistened with sparkling dew.

Golden rays of sunshine cast shadows on the earth below.

Roses awakened to greet the day and spread their intoxicating aroma.

Lavender stalks reached gracefully toward the brightening sky.

Birds sang a cheery tune as they busily prepared for the day.

Lanky tree limbs stretched as if on tiptoe to reach the sun's cascade.

I watched with awestruck wonder as God's creation in all its glorious splendor came together in worship, grateful for a new day. Everything in my yard worshipped the Creator in the way that He had designed. I may not be a flower or a tree, or always smell like a rose, but I can worship God in the unique way that He has created me—my worship can still be a fragrant and pleasing aroma. I will sing aloud in song and thank Him with my breath. I will worship and praise the LORD with every ounce of me.

Psalm 150:6, "Let everything that has breath praise the LORD."

How have you witnessed creation worship our Creator? How can you join in the glorious chorus of praise?

New Lease

Our forgiveness is instantaneous the second we accept Jesus as our Savior and believe in His sacrifice as payment for our sin. The moment we put our faith in Jesus, our sins are wiped completely away, and we stand as a new creation before God. Our newness though is a continual work in progress as we walk with Jesus as our Lord.

Forgiven is our standing before God; being made *new* is our fresh lease on life—ready to follow God and to live according to His will.

I'd like to share a short Bible story about a man named Lazarus. He and his sisters, Mary and Martha, were some of Jesus' best friends. They lived in a town called Bethany which was two miles over the hill from Jerusalem.

Lazarus had fallen ill and was on the verge of death when his sisters sent word for Jesus to come and heal him. Jesus could have rushed right over and kept Lazarus from dying by healing him on the spot. But Jesus took four days before arriving on the scene. By the time He arrived His dear friend Lazarus had died, and it appeared that all hope was lost.

That is where our story takes up now:

John 11:38-44, "Jesus, once more deeply moved, came to the tomb. It was a cave with a stone laid across the entrance. 'Take away the stone,' he said. 'But, Lord,' said Martha, the sister of the dead man, 'by this time there is a bad odor, for he has been there four days.'

Then Jesus said, 'Did I not tell you that if you believe, you will see the glory of God?'

So they took away the stone. Then Jesus looked up and said, 'Father, I thank you that you have heard me. I knew that you always hear me, but I said this for the benefit of the people standing here, that they may believe that you sent me.' When he had said this, Jesus called in a loud voice, 'Lazarus, come out!' The dead man came out, his hands and feet wrapped with strips of linen, and a cloth around his face.

Jesus said to them, **'Take off the grave clothes and let him go.'"**

According to everyone else's timetable Jesus had arrived too late, but as we just read, Jesus is in authority over all things. Hope was resurrected and so too was Lazarus, thanks to the power of God. Lazarus' healing was a two-part process—Jesus raised him from the dead and brought him back to life. Decay no longer had a hold on the formerly deceased man—he was healed, redeemed, and set free. At the command of Jesus, Lazarus came out of the tomb and stood before the crowd still shrouded in his grave clothes. But being that he was no longer dead, his grave clothes were no longer appropriate for him to wear. The time for mourning was over; it was time for celebration. Lazarus was alive! The grave clothes had to come off for him to move freely and enjoy the benefits of his new lease on life. Lazarus was given new life in Christ, but he had to consciously choose to live in that reality.

The same is true for us; Jesus has called us out of the grave and the confines of sin and into the newness of life with Him. The clothes of our old self are no longer appropriate for us to wear. It is time to take off our sin, our shame, our condemnation, our insecurity, our fears—our old self. It is time to embrace the new life He has given us—putting on the righteousness, joy, hope, faith, peace, power, and confidence that are ours in Jesus.

Jesus accomplished part one of our resurrection when He overcame death, walked out of the Tomb, and when He called us by name. We have a huge part to play in the second part of our healing—we must choose to believe it!

We are forgiven and new. That is our identity! It is time we walk, live, and breathe in it!

Have you taken off your grave clothes? Are you fully living in your newness of life in Christ? Ask Jesus to help you do so now.

Days to Come

Life is filled with ups and downs; we daily encounter the predictable and the completely unexpected; things both joyous and painful that have the potential to temporarily take our breath away. This year, much like all others that have come and gone before, has been a mixed bag of both good things and bad. There have been celebration of births and mourning of deaths as well; there have been weddings and divorces. We have endured mass shootings and the wreaking of destruction, and we have also experienced massive outpourings of love resulting in communities healing together. We have seen the violent force of nature that fire can become when it ravages everything in its path. Yet we have also witnessed the bright and hopeful sprouts of green popping up on surrounding hillsides after just the littlest sprinkling of rain. God is with us through it all, nothing escapes His care. He is right beside us on this roller coaster ride. He rejoices with us in our times of joy, and He mourns with us in our times of sorrow. And despite the curves that loom ahead of us, He is never taken by surprise. No matter what we face, He is our steadfast Rock of Salvation and our firm Foundation of Peace. He is our hope eternal and in Him our confidence is secure, not because things in our lives are perfect, but because He continues to be perfectly good to us through it all.

God's love is lavish. His comfort is palpable. His power is endless. His grace is sufficient. Let us pray for His blessing and an awareness of His Almighty Presence in our lives for the year we have ahead. Let us also praise Him and give thanks for every day He gives us.

A Prayer for the days to come:

"May God be gracious to us and bless us and make his face shine on us—so that your ways may be known on earth, your salvation among all nations. May the peoples praise you, God; may all the peoples praise you." Psalm 67:1-3

Add your own prayer here:

No Other

In recent years I enjoyed the blessing of traveling to the Holy Land of Israel. During my pilgrimage, I felt the Bible come to life for me in a fresh and tangible way. Before heading into Israel, our group spent some time across the Jordan River, exploring the land of Jordan. This was an adventure unlike any I had previously experienced. It was a trip filled with amazing quests and brand-new encounters. One of our days was spent at Petra, an archeological wonder of the world. It was incredible to see firsthand the remnants of such an ancient civilization remaining today. Thousands of years ago, people known as the Nabateans were occupants of this city and evidence of their culture still stands. Though the Israelites across the river worshiped the LORD, these people worshiped various gods and had many idols to which they prayed and aimed to appease. As we walked through the Siq—a narrow gorge in Petra—we saw remnants of these gods carved into the rock walls along the way. One of these carvings was of a god who had no mouth, and when we asked our guide why this was the case, he replied that this god did not speak. Fortunately, we serve the one true God who not only speaks, but continually reaches out and pursues communication with the people He has made. Our God has given us the written Word revealing His heart for humanity throughout generations. He did not leave us to fumble around in the dark all alone—He has given us His Holy Spirit, the Holy Bible, and His One and Only Son. He has removed all obstacles to our communication with Him. He invites us to come to Him often in prayer and enjoy sweet fellowship in His Presence. Our God most definitely speaks. We need only listen.

As Christians we do not serve man-made gods, molded, sculpted, or etched by human hands. The God we serve is the Creator of all things. The Lord we call upon is powerfully alive and active. He is beyond anything our human minds could dream up. He reigns from His throne room in Heaven, yet He communicates with His earth-bound children. People have always longed to worship something or someone and have searched in so many dead-end places. The persistent tug in our hearts, the undeniable nudge in our souls is meant to remind us that we were created by God and for God, intended to worship Him alone.

I do not want to place my trust in something I can manufacture with my own two hands. I want to worship the One who created my two hands, cares for my heart, and gives me life.

Deuteronomy 4:39, " know therefore today, and lay it to your heart, that the Lord is God in heaven above and on the earth beneath; there is no other."

What do you notice people putting their trust in? What or who have you been tempted to entrust your faith to? How does knowing that the One True God seeks to communicate with you, lead you to trust and worship Him alone?

Sustainer

If you ever feel forgotten, overlooked, or disregarded, know that the Lord Himself watches over you—every precious second of every single day. If your feet constantly wander and you feel restless in your heart, it is time to stop your searching, settle in, and make your home in the presence of the Savior. If you feel alone and abandoned, without security and guidance, I urge you to seek refuge and find safety in the arms of your Heavenly Father. If you long for love and the intimacy of a relationship, remember that you belong to Jesus, and He calls you His beloved bride.

God watches over you day and night; He is concerned with every detail of your life. You are never ever forgotten in the Lord's eyes.

Psalm 146:9, "The LORD watches over the alien and sustains the fatherless and the widow..."

Have you surrendered to your Sustainer?

Our Future

The moment we place our faith in Jesus Christ as our Savior surrendering to Him as Lord of our life, is the moment we are sealed with God's Holy Spirit, securing our eternal heavenly future with Him. His Spirit comes to dwell in our hearts, comfort our minds, guide our lives, and seal our redemption. His Spirit is a deposit of the good things to come—our blessed inheritance as children of God—in the Kingdom of Heaven.

In Christ we are included, marked, and guaranteed a glorious future with our Heavenly Father—no one can snatch us out of His sovereign hand, or alter His sovereign plan. He promises to be with us each day of our lives and He vows to return from Heaven someday and take us to be with Him always.

We are secure in His love forever. He is sovereign over our future.

We *are God's possession—to the praise of His glory.* Amen.

Ephesians 1:13-14, "And you also were included in Christ when you heard the message of truth, the gospel of your salvation. When you believed, you were marked in him with a seal, the promised Holy Spirit, who is a deposit guaranteeing our inheritance until the redemption of those who are God's possession—to the praise of his glory."

How does this eternal security make you feel?

Our Shield

Most of our battles take place in our minds—we question God's promises, and we forget our identity as a child of God; we give in to our feelings and let insecurity take over and tear us down. Our situations and circumstances, words from others and whispers from Satan can all get in our heads and paralyze us with doubt— unless we *take our thoughts captive* and turn them over to God. He is the One who can shield our heads in the moment, day, week, or season of struggle. If we fill our hearts and minds with Scripture on a regular basis, God will remind us of truth and bring His Word to the surface at the exact instant we need it. He will help us fight off the lies that aim to entrap us by counteracting them with His holy truth. Remembering who God is and who He says we are, is the best shield for our heads in any size skirmish or battle. By reading our Bible we know for a fact that God has already won the war.

Psalm 140:7, "Sovereign Lord, my strong deliverer, you shield my head in the day of battle."

Pause and take a moment to pray and put on your shield today.

Overcome

Lord, help me to overcome the ways of this world with the mindset of Jesus.

Help me to overcome:

The existence of evil with the presence of good.

Acts of hate with deeds of love.

Trembling fear with unwavering faith.

Ulterior motives with pure intentions.

Pits of despair with springs of hope.

Heaviness of heart with unshakable joy.

Discontentment with grateful thanksgiving.

Outer turmoil with inner peace.

Shifting emotions with unchanging truth.

My human weaknesses with the power of Christ.

1 John 5:4-5, *"for everyone born of God overcomes the world. This is the victory that has overcome the world, even our faith. Who is it that overcomes the world? Only the one who believes that Jesus is the Son of God."*

Let's pray: Lord, help me to overcome every obstacle and tendency by leaning into You. Help me to overcome and shine and overflow by the strength of Your Spirit at work in me. Amen.

Reassuring Peace

Snow-balling worries cloud our vision of reality and crowd out our blessings from God. They skew our perception and blow circumstances and concerns beyond what they really are. Once we remember that our God is bigger than anything we could possibly face, our problems quickly shrink down to their proper size. Reflecting on the loving and powerful nature of God, helps us maintain a proper perspective and eases our persistent fears. God graciously offers to replace our anxieties with His reassuring peace. We need only hand them over to His care.

1 Peter 5:6-7, "Humble yourselves, therefore, under God's mighty hand, that he may lift you up in due time. Cast all your anxiety on him because he cares for you."

Where do you need God's reassuring peace today? Are you ready to exchange your anxieties?

Persevering

God is so good to us! He shares with us the secret to strength, courage, and abundant living just as He did with His people long ago. The Lord tells us to be careful to obey His Word and live according to His ways; to keep His Word in our heart and on the tip of our tongue, meditating on it night and day. Let it sink deep into our soul, directing the course of our life. We must remember that the LORD our God is always with us, wherever we go! Whatever battles we face, we never face them alone. God is with each of us every step of the way. Sometimes He will tell us to simply be still as He takes care of our battle all on His own. Often though, He will require that we be a part of the process and put in effort too, building our character, endurance, and faith in the process. We must keep our eyes on Jesus and on the heavenly prize He has promised—always persevering with Jesus in mind. We have a powerful weapon that the people of the Old Testament didn't have—we have God's Spirit dwelling inside!

Joshua 1:7-9, "Be strong and very courageous. Be careful to obey all the law my servant Moses gave you; do not turn from it to the right or to the left, that you may be successful wherever you go. Keep this Book of the Law always on your lips; meditate on it day and night, so that you may be careful to do everything written in it. Then you will be prosperous and successful. Have I not commanded you? Be strong and courageous. Do not be afraid; do not be discouraged, for the LORD your God will be with you wherever you go."

Precise Recipe

Thank you, Lord, for simplifying things and giving us the precise recipe for our redemption. According to Your Holy Word, there is no other name under heaven by which we gain salvation than the Name of Jesus. He alone is the Way, the Truth, and the Life. You have clearly revealed the way to eternal life through Your Son. All other recipes will only direct us away from Your heart and lead us astray from Your love. We do not need to earn our place in Your Kingdom, but only receive the gift You offer. Your recipe for salvation is perfect—equal amounts of justice and mercy, and truth and grace. There is nothing we can add and nothing we should subtract; the tiniest alterations to Your recipe and our salvation falls flat.

We dare not concoct our own formulations; the outcome just would not be the same. We cannot incorporate our own ingredients apart from Your Word, for the taste could never be as sweet. We adjust the preparations in any way, and we get something altogether different than what we desire and what we truly need. Your recipe for our salvation is absolutely perfect, in every single way. I wouldn't change a thing!

You have prepared for me a salvation that I gratefully savor every day.

John 14:6, "Jesus answered, 'I am the way and the truth and the life. No one comes to the Father except through me.'"

How does the beautiful simplicity of God's plan for your salvation free you from the burden of perfection and uncertainty?

Downy Puffs

Every time I turn on the news yet another report of destruction and devastation flashes across the television screen— catastrophic hurricanes, fires, and mud slides. To our human understanding it appears that nature is raging out of control. Fortunately, God consoles our hearts and eases our minds with reminders that He is in command of everything in heaven and on earth. While on an afternoon walk, He drew my attention to the grass below my feet and to the wispy silhouette of a dandelion bending in the breeze. Over the years, this itty-bitty flower has been a sweet reminder for me to pray—not just wishes, but prayers to a God who actually hears me and cares about what I have to say. After stumbling upon this airy, winsome treasure, I reached down and plucked it from the ground, and held it carefully in my hand. Marveling at the intricate and intentional detail of God's tiny creation, I saw order, control, and perfection in its design—giving me further encouragement in the fact that God holds the whole world and me in His capable hands. God not only receives my prayers, but He has the power to act on them too. So, as I walked on, I talked to God about what was on my heart, sharing whatever came to mind. Then I paused briefly in the moment and gently blew the downy puffs into the air, sending my prayers heaven bound.

Psalm 141:2, "May my prayer be set before you like incense; may the lifting up of my hands be like the evening sacrifice."

Take a moment to pray and ask the Lord to remind you that He tenderly hears your prayers, and He powerfully acts on your behalf.

Wonderful

Do you ever wonder if God truly cares? Rest assured, He cares more about you than you can fully comprehend! Scripture gives solid reassurance as to how much the Lord is interested in absolutely every area of your life.

To think that the Lord of Heaven has an interest in my life is beyond my full comprehension. While God powerfully holds the stars in the sky and keeps the world spinning, He also tenderly holds my life in His hands and keeps my heart beating. The Creator of the universe is with *me* every moment of every day—this knowledge is too great for me to fathom. My sovereign God is personally acquainted with all my comings and my goings; there is not a detail of my life of which He is not aware. He is intimately familiar with my thoughts, my actions, and even my failings. He sees every step I take and witnesses every choice I make, and despite myself He still loves me so—such a wonderful notion leaves me breathless and grateful. I am awed by God's glory. I am comforted by His love. I am overwhelmed by His mercy. I am humbled by His grace. I am greatly blessed by His Presence in my life, and cling to the wonderful promise that He will never leave me.

Psalm 139:1-6, "You have searched me, LORD, and you know me. You know when I sit and when I rise; you perceive my thoughts from afar. You discern my going out and my lying down; you are familiar with all my ways. Before a word is on my tongue you, LORD, know it completely. You hem me in behind and before, and you lay your hand upon me. Such knowledge is too wonderful for me, too lofty for me to attain."

How does the wonderful and lofty knowledge of God's nearness and attentiveness affect you? What portion of these Scriptures speak to your heart the most? Why?

Pray with me:

Lord, I am awed by the fact that You know every detail of my life and still love me. You know every thought that passes through my mind and You love me nonetheless, even though I am often quite contrary. You hear every word I speak, both the kind and the hurtful, yet You still bend down low and listen to me. You see my every action, including those of selfish motivation, yet You continue to stick with me and guide me onward. You know me so perfectly well, all my short-comings and my flaws, and yet still pour out Your love and abundantly bless me. The knowledge of Your grace is too lofty for me to fully comprehend, all I know is that I am extremely grateful. Amen.

Over Me

God, You are sovereign over every detail of my life. You are familiar with all my ways and are sovereign over the number of my days. You read my thoughts and are familiar with my ranging emotions—my joys and sufferings are no mystery to You. My past, present, and future are all perfectly laid out before You, for they are a part of Your sovereign plan. You are keenly aware of where I have been, and You know exactly where I am going. There is nowhere I can venture that Your love will not surely follow. There is no sin I can commit that Your grace cannot cover. There is no action I can take or word I can speak that Your extravagant mercy cannot redeem and turn into something that can be used for my good and Your glory. You, O Lord, are sovereign over me.

Your eyes beheld my unformed body, before anyone even anticipated my birth. You lovingly stitched and wove me together in the hidden quiet of my mother's womb. You uniquely created me with Your special touch; no detail was overlooked. Before I even came into this world, every day of my life had been recorded in Your Book. My moments had already been numbered by You—my very first word spoken, my first step taken, my first giggle, my first heartbreak, when I first gave my life to Jesus, and when I will take my first step into Heaven. From the initial beat of my heart and the very first breath I took, to my final pulse and my very last sigh, You have been sovereign over my every step in-between. The course of my life and the span of my lifetime are of no surprise to You. Thus I entrust You with each of my days.

You, O God, are sovereign over me. I trust You with my life here on earth, and for the day when I step into Your Kingdom.

Amen.

Psalm 139:7-16, "Where can I go from your Spirit? Where can I flee from your presence? If I go up to the heavens, you are there; if I make my bed in the depths, you are there. If I rise on the wings of the dawn, if I settle on the far side of the sea, even there your hand will guide me, your right hand will hold me fast. If I say, "Surely the darkness will hide me and the light become night around me," even the darkness will not be dark to you; the night will shine like the day, for darkness is as light to you. For you created my inmost being; you knit me together in my mother's womb. I praise you because I am fearfully and wonderfully made; your works are wonderful, I know that full well. My frame was not hidden from you when I was made in the secret place, when I was woven together in the depths of the earth. Your eyes saw my unformed body; all the days ordained for me were written in your book before one of them came to be."

According to these verses, meditate on the following simple reminders throughout the day and notice the change it makes:

God made me. God loves me.

God has a purpose for my life.

God has a hope for my future.

How does knowing that God is sovereign over every moment of your life and has even traced out each number of your days impact your faith? Describe the peace and comfort this knowledge brings.

Abundantly

I know there is a battle going on in the heavenly places and all around me. The war for my salvation has already been won through the death and resurrection of Jesus my Savior. Although I stand victorious in the war for my soul, I know there is still a battle raging for my faith, joy, peace, and hope. I refuse to wave a white flag of defeat and let Satan have his way. If Jesus paid such an extravagant price to set me free and bestow such abundant blessings, I will stand my ground in the authority of Christ and deny Satan any power over me. The blessings Jesus has given me are meant to be mine for all of eternity and no one has the right to steal them away. I will clutch tightly to Jesus, winning the contest for my faith. The closer my relationship is to Him, the more secure my joy, peace, and hope remain.

John 10:10, "The thief comes only to steal and kill and destroy. I came that they may have life and have it abundantly."

Ask Jesus to help you stand your ground against the enemy today. Cling tightly to Him and claim His promises to you.

Your Glory

Lord, *this is the day that You have made,* and the display of Your Presence is everywhere. I'm going to be mindful of the fact that wherever I go today, You are already there. Your glory speaks through all of creation. The heavens declare Your handiwork; the oceans roar Your fame; the mountains proclaim Your grandeur; the winds gently whisper Your Name. Your heart is spoken through Your children, as Your love and mercy are passed on. When I still my mind and quiet my heart, open my eyes, attune my ears, and simply pay attention, I cannot help but notice evidence of Your Presence abounds all around me. The whole world has joined in song, singing a joyful *Halleluiah*. You call me to be more than merely an observer, You bid me to participate and add my voice to the heavenly chorus of Your praise.

Let all of creation, including me, rejoice for the sake of Your glory today and every day! I pray these things in Jesus' Name. Amen.

Psalm 118:24, "This is the day the LORD has made; We

will rejoice and be glad in it. "NKJV

How do you notice the display of God's Presence today? Join your voice to the heavenly chorus of praise too.

Soul Medicine

Recently I took a day trip to the beach—it was a day of solitude, just me, myself, and I.

I basked in the warm sunshine and felt the cool gentle breeze brush past my face, while under the canopy of a bright blue sky. It was a time of much needed refreshment for my soul. The day did not disappoint in the slightest. I sunk my toes in the sand, let the waves lap over my legs, soaked up the sun on my skin, and listened as sounds of laughter echoed over the roar of the tide. I saw the Lord's goodness everywhere—birds diving into the deep, sand crabs skittering across the golden sand. There were children joyfully darting in and out of the waves as if playing a game of tag, protective parents relaxing nearby, and dolphins putting on a show as they blissfully surfed on by. A day out in nature, enjoying the Lord's creation in the company of my Creator, was the medicine my soul desperately needed.

Proverbs 17:22, "A cheerful heart is good medicine, but a crushed spirit dries up the bones."

Reflect on a time when the Lord cheered your soul. Where were you and what were you doing?

Seek First

Jesus wisely exhorts us to seek Him and His Kingdom first, giving Him priority over everything else in our lives—even above ourselves and our loved ones. He promises that by seeking Him first everything else we need in this life will be added to us.

We gain a new heavenly perspective by seeking Jesus and His Kingdom first; He aligns our desires and our minds to His heart and prioritizes our lives according to His will.

When we seek Jesus first, contentment fills our hearts, our endless strivings cease, our obsession with money and worldly possessions takes a backseat—instead of being our idol, they become rather an end to our means of serving each other. Our homes become places of hospitality and invitation, of safety and refuge where others are always welcome. When we give Jesus His rightful place in our lives, our worries, our fears, our judgements, jealousies, and world views fall by the wayside. With Him as our focus, our purpose comes into view with new-found clarity.

Everything we have—the breath in our lungs, the words on our tongues, the roof over our heads, and the ability of our hands, all comes from and belongs to Jesus, and are meant to be used for His Kingdom. Our blessings are meant to be enjoyed and held loosely, keeping in mind that we are merely stewards of all the gifts that our Lord gives.

The Bible tells us to seek Jesus first, last, and always.

Jesus is on the Throne and He has our life in His loving hands.

Matthew 6:32-34, "If that is how God clothes the grass of the field, which is here today and tomorrow is thrown into the fire, will he not much more clothe you—you of little faith? So do not worry, saying, 'What shall we eat?' or 'What shall we drink?' or 'What shall we wear?' For the pagans run after all these things, and your heavenly Father knows that you need them. But seek first his kingdom and his righteousness, and all these things will be given to you as well. Therefore do not worry about tomorrow, for tomorrow will worry about itself. Each day has enough trouble of its own."

What have you tended to seek after first—what have you given priority in your life? Ask Jesus to help you reprioritize, making Him your number One pursuit.

Sovereign Plan

God sovereignly created the heavens and the earth, and He has held them in their place throughout the ages. He sovereignly created you and me, as He lovingly knit and wove us together in the safety of our mothers' wombs. He knows the hairs on our heads, and He sovereignly ordains our days. He saw the great chasm that sin brought into the world and how it separated His beloved creation from the glory of His Presence—and His heart broke at the severed condition of our relationship with Him. He knew that there was no way for mankind to possibly right itself with Him, so He sovereignly sent His Own Son to bear the burden for us all. Jesus came to pay the ultimate price for your sin and mine. He gave His life as a sacrifice for all who would believe in His Name. Jesus' death on the Cross was no surprise to our Heavenly Father—it was His sovereignly orchestrated plan from before time even began. Jesus Christ, our Lord and Savior purposefully came to set us free from the curse of sin and the threat of death. He sovereignly invites each of us to take our place in His eternal Heavenly Kingdom. No one else, past, present, or future has the power to save—our God is the God who sovereignly saves.

God alone is our Savior as these following verses proclaim:

Psalm 68:19-21, "Praise be to the Lord, to God our Savior, who daily bears our burdens. Our God is a God who saves; from the Sovereign LORD comes escape from death."

I have visited the place and seen the actual steps that Jesus traversed as He was led to Caiaphas the high priests' house where

He faced accusations that would lead to His death. After an evening spent celebrating the Passover Supper with His disciples and praying in the Garden of Gethsemane, Jesus, heavy-hearted, walked from the Garden across the Kidron Valley, up the steps to the hillside where He endured His first trial. Although Jesus was led by His captors, He was ultimately in control of the situation. He could have called on the angels of Heaven to save Him, but He purposefully walked this path and bore this burden for you and me. He is sovereign in all things.

Jesus' life was not taken from Him—He freely gave it to set us free.

Pause and reflect on all that Jesus endured for your salvation. What emotions well up in your heart?

A Season

King Solomon accurately and wisely assessed that *there is a time for everything, and a season for every activity under the heavens.* There is significant purpose in both the difficult and easy seasons of life—the hard times refine us and teach us, and make the good times seem that much more precious. We rejoice when a baby is born, and we reflect on a life that has passed. We sow seeds in anticipation of the harvest to come, and then at the end of the season notice how the dirt lays barren. We put to death the things that harm us, and then allow a period for our hearts to heal. We tear down lies and strongholds, and we build up truth in our minds. We weep in times of sorrow, and we also have reasons to smile, giggle, and laugh. We deeply mourn our losses, and we joyfully celebrate our achievements. As a result of the 2020 pandemic, we greatly appreciate the time for hugging and respect the time for keeping at arm's length. We hold our tongues from tearing others down, and we use our words to bless and build others up. We love the righteous things of the Lord but hate the evil of this world.

There is an appropriate time and season for everything under the sun. If we look intently, we will notice the Lord's hand is at work through it all.

Ecclesiastes 3:1-8, "There is a time for everything, and a season for every activity under the heavens:

a time to be born and a time to die, a time to plant and a time to uproot, a time to kill and a time to heal, a time to tear down and a time to build, a time to weep and a time to laugh, a time to mourn and a time to dance, a time to scatter stones and a time to gather them, a time to embrace and a time to refrain from embracing, a time to search and a time to give up, a time to keep and a time to throw away, a time to tear and a time to mend, a time to be silent and a time to speak, a time to love and a time to hate, a time for war and a time for peace."

How does knowing that God has a purpose for everything, and that He is with you through every season encourage you to persevere?

How have difficult times made your good times seem more precious?

Stay Close

I often witness God's Word and His illustrations come alive in my own circumstances. Early one morning I opened the back door to let my dog out into the yard for a moment. I had barely turned to grab a cup of coffee from the kitchen, when out of the corner of my eye I saw my small, gentle-natured dog climbing the steep slope up toward the wrought iron fence edging our yard. As I focused more intently, I noticed that my naïve dog was nose-to-nose with a sizeable, strong, and healthy coyote, who was staring him down as if ready to gobble him up. (This wasn't my dog's first encounter with a coyote, but hopefully it was his last.) Quick as a flash—well, as fast as I could manage—I climbed the hill to rescue my dog. I got about halfway up and called to my dog, commanding him to come back down by my side. After much coercing he finally did, though the coyote lingered hoping to catch my dog once again all alone. My husband later asked me if I had planned to fight the coyote off, and I told him that if needed, I would have. My dog put himself in jeopardy by wandering from me and disobeying my voice.

Like my dog we behave in much the same way. We stray from our Master's side, wander off into danger, and unfortunately we too have an enemy roaming and seeking to devour us. The coyote I faced off with didn't even flinch when I approached—apparently, I wasn't a very threatening adversary to it. A huge difference between my furry friend's situation and ours is that when God stands up in our defense, the devil trembles in terror and quickly flees. God is our powerful defender; He is our loving protector and mighty rescuer. He is our blessed Savior. It is in our best interest to continually stay close to the Lord, but in those unfortunate instances when we wander away, we must remember to loudly call on His Name. The Lord acts in our defense and the wily devil takes his leave.

1 Peter 5:8, "Be alert and of sober mind. Your enemy the devil prowls around like a roaring lion looking for someone to devour."

James 4:7, "Submit yourselves, then, to God. Resist the devil, and he will flee from you."

Psalm 91:14, ""Because he loves me," says the LORD, "I will rescue him; I will protect him, for he acknowledges My Name."

Were you aware that the enemy prowls and seeks to devour you? How does knowing that the Lord is your defender encourage you to stay close to Him and call on His Name in times of danger?

Still Blessed

My life is filled with many blessings, but I count my relationship with Jesus as the greatest of them all. Even if everything else was stripped away, I would still be blessed because I have Him and I know I always will.

Jesus is where my hope is found despite uncertain circumstances. I cling to the promise of eternity with Jesus in Heaven and to the knowledge that He is constantly here with me on earth. My hope is securely established in the reassuring perspective He gives me.

He is where my joy is found even in difficult situations. Happiness comes and goes depending on the day or even the moment, but my joy is deeply rooted in things beyond the surface where it cannot be stolen or much less shaken. My joy springs forth from within my heart, where Jesus now resides.

He is where I find my peace even amid the rocky places. I keep my eyes locked on Him and trust that He has everything under complete control. I know that whatever the outcome, Jesus will use it for His glory and my ultimate growth. He is my peace in the stillness and in every single storm.

He is where I find my rest when I am utterly worn out. He wipes my brow and refreshes my soul. He breathes fresh life to my weary bones. He speaks tenderly to me and calms my restless heart. To receive this rest though, I must remember to stop and spend time with Him on a regular basis.

Jesus is the source of all my blessings—they begin and end with Him. My blessings are found when I firmly plant my feet on His promises and anchor my faith solidly to Him. No matter what awaits me around the corner, I will press on knowing that I am still blessed. And nothing and no one can take that blessing way.

Job 1:21, "And he said, 'Naked I came from my mother's womb, and naked shall I return. The LORD gave, and the LORD has taken away; blessed be the name of the LORD.'"

How has your relationship with Jesus been your greatest blessing?

Sufficient

Grace. Grace. Grace.

One simple word to perfectly sum up our lives in Christ.

By grace we have everything we will ever require.

By grace our hearts beat and our lungs breathe, both supplying us life.

By grace we receive forgiveness for our sin through the sacrifice of Jesus.

By grace we start afresh each morning, washed clean from the previous day.

By grace we approach God's throne with confidence.

By grace we are the hands and feet of Jesus, serving those in need.

By grace we are the healing balm of the Savior, speaking His words of hope and comfort to the downhearted.

By grace we are instruments in the Kingdom of Heaven, representing the King on earth.

By grace we hold our tongues from speaking words of harshness.

By grace we turn from our selfish motives and pursue selfless acts of kindness.

By grace we seek unity, love, and understanding despite our differences.

By grace we have God's peace, and by grace we share His peace with others.

By grace we abound in joy, and by grace joy overflows from us.

By grace we walk in faith, and by grace we lead others to find faith in Jesus.

By grace we are victorious over life and death.

By grace we are strong, knowing that God walks with us through the valleys.

By grace we sing praise from the mountaintops.

By grace we worship at the Lord's feet.

Grace, a word that surrounds us, fills us, leads us, and lifts us.

God's grace is sufficient for all that we need. His grace is at work in us.

Amen.

2 Corinthians 12:9, "But he [the Lord] said to me, 'My grace is sufficient for you, for my power is made perfect in weakness.' Therefore, I will boast all the more gladly about my weaknesses, so that Christ's power may rest on me."

List the ways you have found the Lord's grace to be sufficient in your life.

Supreme

As a member of the Holy Trinity and a blessed part of the Godhead, Jesus Christ is the supreme authority over all of creation—things in heaven above and on the earth below; things we can see with our naked eye, things of microscopic size, and things of the spiritual world that escape our sight. Jesus is supreme over life and death, and over every person to ever walk this planet whether they acknowledge Him or not. He is supreme over every believer who has placed their faith in Him and accepted His sacrifice on their behalf. He is our supreme peacemaker—bringing peace between mankind and our Heavenly Father.

Jesus is the supreme hope of the world.
The word *"sovereign"* means *supreme in power and authority*.

Colossians 1:15-23, "The Son is the image of the invisible God, the firstborn over all creation. For in him all things were created: things in heaven and on earth, visible and invisible, whether thrones or powers or rulers or authorities; all things have been created through him and for him. He is before all things, and in him all things hold together. And he is the head of the body, the church; he is the beginning and the firstborn from among the dead, so that in everything he might have the supremacy. For God was pleased to have all his fullness dwell in him, and through him to reconcile to himself all things, whether things on earth or things in heaven, by making peace through his blood, shed on the cross. Once you were alienated from God and were enemies in your minds because of your evil behavior. But now he has reconciled you by Christ's physical body through death to present you holy in his sight, without blemish and free from accusation—if you continue in your faith, established and firm, and do not move from the hope held out in the gospel. This is the gospel that you heard and that has been proclaimed to every creature under heaven, and of which I, Paul, have become a servant."

We can maintain a mindset of peace and hold onto our sense of joy by believing that Jesus is sovereign over everything. What do you need to trust Jesus with today?

Take Heart

Our quest for peace is often misdirected and misplaced. We seek the tranquil and quiet, undisturbed and undemanding, restful and carefree—we pursue the just out-of-reach notion of what we think peace should be. Invariably, people and circumstances will intrude the veneer of our serenity and try to shake our foundation and disrupt our peace, and far too often they succeed. So long as our peace is wrapped up in the unstable and ever-changing world around us our bliss will continue to be at risk. Our peace must be wrapped in the arms of our Ever-Lasting Savior.

Our idea of peace runs contrary to what Jesus teaches. Peace is attainable not by the absence of chaos in the world, but through Jesus who overcame it for us. Peace is not the omission of tribulations; it is the Presence of Jesus in our trials! That is His promise we cling to! So, dear friend take heart!

John 14:27, "Peace I leave with you; my peace I give you. I do not give to you as the world gives. Do not let your hearts be troubled and do not be afraid."

John 16:33, "I have told you these things, so that in me you may have peace. In this world you will have trouble. But take heart! I have overcome the world."

How have you experienced Jesus' peace even in turbulent times?

Give Thanks

God is faithful even when we are faithless. He pours out blessings even though we forget to give thanks. He is good to us even when we are a bit rotten. He extends grace even though we have done nothing to earn it. He lavishes us with love even in the moments when we are not so lovable. God is perfect and accepts us despite our imperfections. He makes us right with Himself, when on our own we go, oh so wrong. He does all of this through His blessed Son Jesus. All I can say is, "Thank You, Lord!"

Psalm 106:1, "Praise the LORD. Give thanks to the LORD, for he is

good; his love endures forever."

Use this space to offer the Lord your own thanks:

Grateful Response

Thanksgiving is a mindset that we are meant to carry with us all year long. It never goes out of season—it's not just for the autumn when the leaves turn to brilliant shades of red, but for the long cold dark nights of winter, the vibrant days of spring, and the warm leisure of summer months too. God showers us with blessings and provisions not just one day out of the year, but each and every day that passes. Whatever season we are currently in, our thanksgiving should pour out to the Lord in grateful response. It is always the right time to praise His holy Name and tell of His wonderful deeds.

Psalm 9:1, "I will give thanks to you, Lord, with all my heart; I will tell of all your wonderful deeds."

How can thanksgiving become a yearlong mindset for you?

What wonderful deeds has the Lord done for you? Who can you share your praise-filled testimony with?

Thankfully Aware

Occasionally folks come along and snatch our blessings right out from under us. They grab our joy, peace, and hope and carry them far away. Often though, we are the real culprit who steals our own blessings. We hinder and deny ourselves much of the goodness that God wants to pour into our lives.

We let circumstances dictate our contentment—we allow our own bad attitude to steal our joy, we allow interruptions to disrupt our peace, and we allow obstacles to squash our hope. *We allow* is the pivotal phrase in all these statements.

You see, we have a choice as to whether we remain filled with joy, peace, and hope, or not. It is our choice to allow ourselves to be rattled and shaken or to continue walking steadfastly grounded in the Presence of the Lord. God is continually pouring His goodness into our lives, but it is our choice as to whether *we allow* our blessings to be eclipsed by our difficulties or continue to let the light of gratitude shine in our hearts and minds. Let's be alert and on the lookout, ready to thwart the times of doubt and discouragement, by continually and consciously being thankfully aware, giving thanks to the Lord.

Hebrews 12:28, "Therefore, since we are receiving a kingdom that cannot be shaken, let us be thankful, and so worship God acceptably with reverence and awe..."

Moving forward, how will you be more conscious in what you allow to frame your thoughts and mind? Take a moment now to be thankfully aware.

The Best Place

The path of a joyous life both begins and ends with Jesus. Too often we seek pleasures of the worldly kind to fill our deepest longings. Jesus knows that our pursuits are only in vain—He knows that our heart's true desire and every treasure of eternal value are found within the shadow of His Presence. Every need, every void, and every yearning meets its complete and perfect fulfillment in Him alone. The pleasures He offers are not temporary, they are made to last for all of eternity. Being with Jesus, now and forever, is absolutely the best place we could possibly be.

While I am grateful for my earthly blessings, they were never intended to complete me. I find my joy and contentment in the Presence of the Lord. I will pursue Jesus with all my being.

Psalm 16:11, *"You make known to me the path of life; you will fill me with joy in your presence, with eternal pleasures at your right hand."*

What joyously eternal pleasures have you found in the Presence of the Lord?

Perfect Measure

Lord, Your *power* causes me to tremble and shake;

Your *love* invites me to surrender and rest.

My security in You is founded on both—

Your *power and love* are perfectly blended together.

Without Your *love*, Your *power* would only scare me.

Without Your *power*, Your *love* could not defend me.

Your *power* and *love* combined, create the sweetest recipe.

And a heart full of confidence is the blessing that they bring.

Thank You for being the perfect measure of both!

Your *power* and *love*, they comfort me.

Psalm 59:16, "But I will sing of your strength, in the morning I will sing of your love; for you are my fortress, my refuge in times of trouble."

How are you encouraged by the perfectly balanced combination of God's power and love?

The Door

Each of us has a door to our hearts. We have a choice as to what and who we let enter in. Too often we shut and lock our hearts completely for fear of being hurt. Or we hesitantly keep the door just slightly ajar, cautiously inspecting anyone who dares come near the threshold. The prospect of opening the door completely is one that leaves us vulnerable and exposed. Jesus stands outside the door—He is knocking and beckoning us to open our hearts to Him. There is no need for apprehension, no reason to delay, swing the door wide open and invite Him in to stay.

Revelation 3:20, "Here I am! I stand at the door and knock. If anyone hears my voice and opens the door, I will come in and eat with that person, and they with me."

How would you describe the door to your heart at this moment? Is it open to others? Is it open to the Lord?

The Invitation

Jesus invites us, saying, *"I have a seat saved especially for you. Just plop yourself down and let's have a heart-to-heart chat."*

Amid our busyness Jesus sits and He patiently waits. He observes our hectic schedule, watching us rush here and there to the point of near exhaustion. He knows what we need, and He offers us rest—He invites us to come, and He waits for our response. If only we would look up long enough to catch sight of Him, we would notice Him beckoning us to cease our running, to still our frenzy, to sit by His side. The seat beside Jesus is so much more than a spot to park our frame; it is a place to lay our burdens down and receive His calming peace. The space beside Jesus is where our minds can be quieted, our hearts find their comfort, our lives find their direction, and our priorities fall in line. The seat beside Jesus is place of restoration for our weary bodies; it is a wellspring of refreshment for our thirsty souls. The seat beside Jesus is a sanctuary where we meet face-to-face with the Lord Himself.

Jesus continually extends this invitation to you and to me. And untold blessings pour out when we act on His prompting.

So, as we go through our busy day, let's purposefully look up now and then, listen for Jesus' voice, and watch for His invitation. We do not want to miss out and this beautiful respite!

Matthew 11:28, "Come to me, all you who are weary and burdened, and I will give you rest."

I hope this devotion is just the beginning of your visit with Jesus today.

By Faith

The Lord is sovereign even when I don't understand, and things don't make much sense. His ways are much higher than my ways, so I must choose to trust.

Everything I see in part will someday be fully known—until that day when all is revealed, I will choose to trust.

When I see good people die and bad people thrive, I will choose to trust.

When I see righteousness dwindle and evil seems to take over, even then I will choose to trust.

I will believe and trust, not in my circumstances, but in the Person and character of God. I will trust in His written Word which is *active and alive and sharper than any two-edged sword.*

I choose to believe and trust and walk by faith, knowing that God is loving and His plans for me and this world He created are just and good.

He is working all things for His sovereign purpose, conforming His children into the likeness of His Son. Even when the holy process of being refined is uncomfortable and anything but fun, I will choose to follow and obey and trust in His ways.

Until the moment when Jesus returns and makes everything clear, I will choose to press on toward that glorious Day and trust in His promise to make all things new. I will cling to the hope of my heavenly future with Him. I will walk by faith!

2 Corinthians 5:6-11, "Therefore we are always confident and know that as long as we are at home in the body we are away from the Lord. For we live by faith, not by sight. We are confident, I say, and would prefer to be away from the body and at home with the Lord. So we make it our goal to please him, whether we are at home in the body or away from it. For we must all appear before the judgment seat of Christ, so that each of us may receive what is due us for the things done while in the body, whether good or bad."

How is the Lord calling you to walk by faith and not by sight these days?

Fortify

Acts 16:24-26, "When he received these orders, he put them in the inner cell and fastened their feet in the stocks. About midnight Paul and Silas were praying and singing hymns to God, and the other prisoners were listening to them. Suddenly there was such a violent earthquake that the foundations of the prison were shaken. At once all the prison doors flew open, and everyone's chains came loose."

Many of our circumstances and environments seem like extremely unlikely places to worship. Think of Paul and Silas, imprisoned and mistreated, locked behind bars, with shackles on their feet, in the recesses of a dark, dank cell. It seems like worry, panic, desperation, depression, and hopelessness would be the likely response to their position. As much as I would like to think otherwise, I am quite sure one of those would be mine. But these mighty men of faith chose a different mind-set and got some miraculous results. Instead of fretting, they chose to praise. They overcame fear with songs and prayer; they focused on the Lord, not their situation. Although in chains, their hearts were free, nothing could hold them down. Their prayer and praise helped to fortify their very own souls. And the way they responded to their desperate circumstances was a great testimony to everyone else around. Their songs and prayers gave glory to God, and showed others that despite the way things looked, they still had an amazing hope that nothing and no one could take away. Time passed and their perseverant faith paid off—the Lord released them from the shackles that previously had them bound, and on top of that He opened the iron prison gates and really set them free.

Do you want this kind of faith—the kind that praises and prays, instead of panics? I know I do. Like Paul and Silas, let's choose to overcome our fear with worship; let's focus on the Lord and ask Him to fortify our souls. Let's give glory to God and joyfully share with others the hope we have in Jesus.

Take a moment and ask the Lord to fortify your soul with worship of Him. Ask Him to help you respond with prayer and praise the next time you find yourself in overwhelming situations.

Wild Grace

We often think that if we only had more strength, more energy, more influence, more power, more resolve, or more perfection that we would be able to persevere; we would be better equipped to endure and overcome our situations, our tendencies, and our weaknesses. All that is really needed is for us to realize and grasp the access we have to God's abundant grace, and what that truly means for our lives.

God's grace is sufficient for all our needs—both great and small. Grace is God's unmerited, undeserved favor upon our lives. Grace is our entrance into God's Heavenly Throne Room, our access to His love, His power, and His glorious Presence. The Lord's grace gives us peace in the present moment and assures our eternal hope for the future; it is the basis for our unshakable joy despite circumstances. Grace is a gift from God, poured out for us by way of Jesus Christ. Grace is the arms of Jesus outstretched for you and me; outstretched on the Cross for our salvation; outstretched in welcome as we are invited to take our place in His Divine Kingdom; outstretched, beckoning us to join Him for eternity.

God's magnificent grace is beyond our wildest imaginings, and fortunately it is within our reach. His grace is available and sufficient for our every need. Let's stop depending on ourselves alone and ask God for help and seize His gracious gift.

2 Corinthians 12:9, "My grace is sufficient, for My power is made perfect in weakness."

What do you need God's wild grace for today?

Unchanging

If we hope in things that are not based on the promises of God or founded on God himself, then we are left to battle with feelings of doubt.

If we hope in the Lord God above, the Maker of heaven and earth, then all our fears and worries are appeased, and our hope is firm and secure.

God is unchanging—the same yesterday, today, and tomorrow.

He placed the stars in the sky and calls them to shine each night.

He has established the times and the seasons; He ordains the dusk and the dawn.

He places parameters around us for our own protection and for the sake of our own good.

The Lord is perfect, holy, righteous, loving, merciful, gracious, and kind, and everything He does represents His divine nature.

His character is perfect, faithful, and unchanging.

In God alone our hope is unshaken. In Him alone our confidence is assuredly found.

Psalm 74:16-17, "The day is yours, and yours also the night; you established the sun and moon. It was you who set all the boundaries of the earth; you made both summer and winter."

How does knowing God establishes the sun and moon, affirm your confidence in Him?

Unfailing Love

Lord, each day that passes is a brand new testimony to Your unfailing love for me. You tuck me in tight each night and watch over me as I sleep. You turn the nightlight on and leave it glimmering in the dark sky. You awaken me with the joyous brilliance of a glorious dawn. There is not a day or night—past, present, or future—that You are not watching over me. I know that You are faithful, and Your ways are perfectly just. I believe that You desire the best for me out of all that life has to offer. I daily choose to rest in your promises and trust in your plans for my life. I long to follow you and walk with you all my blessed days. Being with you blesses my soul and is my absolute favorite place to be.

Lord, help me not to stray, but always stay safe by your side. Please teach me which trails to follow, which forks in the road to take, and which bridges to cross as my journey with You unfolds. Wherever the path may wander or meander, may the road continually lead me closer to You. May I dwell in Your Presence and press into Your unfailing love forever. Amen.

Psalm 143:8, "Let the morning bring me word of your unfailing love, for I have put my trust in you. Show me the way I should go, for to you I entrust my life."

What does God's unfailing love mean to you?

Unhurried

The Lord has extended an invitation for you and me to personally know Him better, in the hopes that we will eagerly accept. God asks us step out of our busyness and be fully present in our encounters with Him. He asks us to choose an *unhurried* mindset as we enter His holy Presence, pushing all other thoughts aside. God knows the blessings that will flow as result of our *unhurried* time with Him—our hearts will become more settled, and peace will take over our souls. He knows we will come away from these times of intimacy overwhelmed with faith and hope. We will come away trusting and knowing that He has everything under His loving and sovereign control.

Please read the following as the Lord's personal invitation to you:

Dear Child, take time to savor your quiet moments with Me. Come to Me often and at an unhurried pace. Talk to Me as your loving Father and as your closest Friend; listen to My calming voice and hear My words of guidance; rest in My arms and find shelter in My Presence. I invite you to know and understand Me better—I will never leave, forsake, or disappoint You. I ask you to make unhurried your new frame of mind, especially when it comes to spending time with Me. You will notice that an unexpected additional blessing you receive from our unhurried visits, is that an unhurried pace will naturally overflow into your life overall as well. I invite you to pause, rest, and be unhurried with me.

Love, your Lord and Savior

Psalm 16:11, "You make known to me the path of life; you will fill me with joy in your presence, with eternal pleasures at your right hand."

Trust

It is honestly hard to trust someone we do not know very well. Just as our relationships with other people require time, authenticity, and intimacy, these are vital for growing our trust in the Lord too. If we want to trust God more fully, we must spend time in His Presence and in His Word more regularly. Through this act of communication, we will get to know Him increasingly more, and we will witness His love, faithfulness, and power come to life for us firsthand. Our initial step into a relationship with God is one of trust—trust that Jesus alone can save. This initial choice of faith forever changes the trajectory of our lives. From that moment on, growing our trust in the Lord happens one faith-filled step at a time—building in momentum and intensity as we go along. The more we trust God, the more He proves Himself to be completely trustworthy, inspiring our trust even more.

Psalm 9:10, "Those who know your name trust in you, for you, LORD,

have never forsaken those who seek you."

How have you seen God prove His trustworthiness in your life? How does this inspire you to trust Him more and more?

Universal Hope

No matter where we live or what language we speak, the Gospel Message remains the same: Jesus is King of Glory and Savior of the whole wide world. The hope held out through the Gospel is universal. Whoever places their faith in Jesus and acknowledges that His death on the Cross was a sacrifice given to cover their personal transgressions, is forgiven of their sins, made right with God the Father, and given the hope of eternity in Heaven.

Every spring we take time to celebrate Easter, which along with Christmas is one of the three most important days in the Christian faith. You see, the Friday before Easter is equally important—without Jesus' sacrifice on the Cross for our sins, His resurrection would have no personal impact for us. When Jesus stepped out of the grave He brought us the hope of new life, but first He had to die on the Cross to set us free from our old self. On the Friday proceeding Easter Sunday, Jesus gave His life to free us from sin and defeat the devil on our behalf. That is why the saddest day in history is called *Good Friday*! And that is why we celebrate the combined power of His death and resurrection! Together they offer the universal hope of the world!

Romans 3:22-24, "This righteousness is given through faith in Jesus Christ to all who believe. There is no difference between Jew and Gentile, for all have sinned and fall short of the glory of God, and all are justified freely by his grace through the redemption that came by Christ Jesus."

How has Jesus' sacrifice impacted your eternal and daily hope?

Warfare

There is no greater warfare than worship. When the enemy attacks, whether with doubt, fear, anxiety, depression, anger, or bitterness, our best defense and offense is to turn up the praise! Nothing will send the enemy running quicker than hearing us sing glory to the Name of Jesus. When those discouragements pop in our heads, it is best to head them off immediately. If you have a playlist of favorite songs, blast them and sing along. Through the act of worship, we submit our hearts and draw near to God, and in the process the enemy turns on his heels and flees. The pain that sears his ears is just too unbearable for him to stay. Beginning the morning with worship sets the mood for the whole day ahead—play it while you're getting dressed, or making breakfast and the bed, and see the difference it makes. Play your worship music throughout the day to recalibrate your mindset and keep negative thoughts at bay. Play it while working, or walking, or driving carpool and notice the joy that settles in. Calm your mind and prepare yourself for sweet dreams by softly playing worship music as you climb into bed. Whether day or night, worship songs push away the darkness, while drawing in the Light.

Psalm 95:6-7, "Come, let us bow down in worship, let us kneel before the LORD our Maker; for he is our God and we are the people of his pasture, the flock under his care."

How have you experienced a lift in your spirits and seen the darkness pushed away as a result of turning to worship before?

Honeycomb

Our words have great power, to bring blessing or harm. Let's use them wisely for the purpose of good, to build up and encourage one another, instead of tearing each other down. Words spoken in love taste sweet on the tongue, whereas words spoken is anger taste bitter in our mouth. Words spoken in kindness bring healing to the heart and revive a hurting soul, whereas words spoken in haste can inflict pain and leave a lasting scar. When we open our mouths, let's be sure to speak sentiments of love and kindness. Let's share our faith, joy, and hope which will undoubtedly leave behind the lingering flavor of grace, much like a trace of honeycomb.

Proverbs 16:24, "Gracious words are a honeycomb, sweet to the soul and healing to the bones."

Lord, may the meditations of my mind be set upon Jesus and everything that is pure and beneficial. May I be filled up with Your goodness and then overflow—being a vessel of blessing in this world to everyone who comes across my path. I pray that my words are spoken with Your love and grace, bringing sweet healing to everyone's soul. May my speech bring honor to Your Holy Name.

Amen.

Who?

Oftentimes our circumstances cause us to ask God, *why*?

Maybe we need to stop asking *why* and instead ask questions that focus on *who.*

Who holds the stars in the sky?

Who keeps the earth spinning both day and night?

Who created me and knit me together and numbers all my days?

Who sees my struggles and calls me by name?

Who never leaves me or forsakes me, but stays by my side?

Who uses everything for my good and gives me a hope and a future?

Who is loving, gracious, merciful, and powerful all the time?

Who is my Father—whose daughter am I?

Who is the One who tells me I matter?

God is the One who does all of this and more. He is our sovereign Creator and our loving Heavenly Father. If He says we matter, then we most definitely do. That should give our confidence a boost.

Even if we don't have all the answers or know all the reasons why, we do know that God is good and His plan for us is too.

God sees us all the time; we just need to realize that He is beside us, and pray that He opens our eyes to the blessings He provides.

Genesis 16:13, "She gave this name to the LORD who spoke to her: 'You are the God who sees me,' for she said, 'I have now seen the One who sees me.'"

Do you know that God sees you, and hears you, and cares about you? He does!

How can focusing on God and His promises, and remembering your God-given identity help you more confidently face your circumstances?

With God

On my own I need to feel in control; but with God I can simply and confidently surrender.

When I let my concerns swirl into worries, it's not long before I begin to panic; but when I come to God in prayer, I am filled with a peace that passes all understanding.

My mind can sometimes wander and lead me in many directions; but when I allow God to direct my thoughts, my purpose becomes suddenly clear.

When left to my own defenses I grow weary and overwhelmed; but with God my soul is revived, and I am strong beyond belief.

When I try to navigate life on my own, I can sometimes get a little lost; but with God leading the way before me, the path plainly unfolds.

I can be a bit disheartened when things don't go the way I imagined; but remembering that God's plans for me are good, lifts my spirits and makes my soul contented.

When I remember my own sinful words and actions, regret can start to cloud up my mind; but with God as my Savior, I am washed with grace and given fresh mercies that set me free.

When I focus on myself, selfishness can easily take hold; but with God on the throne, humility and selflessness begin to make me over.

Led by my own heart, love is sometimes easier to withhold; but with God's love flowing through me, it is extravagant and sacrificial.

From my own vantage point, the hills before me seem impossible to summit; but with God, I know that all things are possible, and that includes moving mountains.

Matthew 19:26, "Jesus looked at them and said, 'With man this is impossible, but with God all things are possible.'"

How have you seen God turn the *impossible* into the *possible* in your own life?

Counting Blessings

Far too often our awareness of the blessings that surround us is dimmed by the difficult circumstances we face. Our focus zooms in on all that is going wrong, eclipsing our view of all that is going right. Despite hardships, God is always at work. Let's step back and open our eyes to the abundant blessings God has put in our lives. Let us be present in this very moment, taking notice and counting all the blessings He has already lavished upon us and all that He continues to pour out. Let's ask Him to reveal them to us so that we can give Him thanks. In the process of recounting our blessings and praising our Lord, our spirits get lifted and our hearts get filled. Thanksgiving is an official day for *thanks*, but for our own benefit and to the glory of God, gratitude is meant to be a part of every day. Happy Thanksgiving all year long!

1 Thessalonians 5:18, "Give thanks in all circumstances; for this is God's will for you in Christ Jesus."

You can use this space to count your blessings in this present moment and pour out your own thanks to the Lord:

A Harvest

Gratitude changes everything and everyone.

Planting seeds of gratitude produces an abundant harvest of blessings, with more than enough to go around. Gratitude breathes fresh joy into the air. It warms and reassures our hearts. It brings clarity of sight to our eyes—it alters our perspective with optimistic hope. It washes a settled contentment over our lives. Gratitude positively affects everyone fortunate enough to be caught up in its path.

Appreciation, gratitude, and thanks—words to live by; words that give abundant life.

Colossians 3:16, "Let the message of Christ dwell among you richly as you teach and admonish one another with all wisdom through psalms, hymns, and songs from the Spirit, singing to God with gratitude in your hearts."

How have you seen gratitude change your perspective and mindset before?

Begin each day with a moment of thanksgiving. Close each day with a pause of gratitude for all that the Lord has done.

Heart and Home

It is two weeks before Thanksgiving and I have already begun decorating my home for Christmas—the tree stands tall in the corner; it glimmers and shines brilliantly, illuminating the room with sparkly lights. Its evergreen color brings the woodsy feel of the forest inside. A *Cranberry and Winter Cherry* hand soap sits at the edge of the sink, adding the sweet fragrance of joy to the task of handwashing. The warm aroma of Christmas trees fills the air as a *Frasier Fir* candle crackles and burns. A wreath hangs on the front door as a symbol of welcome to all who approach and serves as an invitation during the blessed holiday season. A small Nativity scene is prominently placed on the center of our coffee table—albeit it stays there all year round.

Jesus is the center of the Christmas Season and every day thereafter. My home has little sprinklings of Christmas throughout and gives an inkling as to the condition of my heart.

Dear Lord, as my heart is a place of joyful celebration, so too may my home be as well. As my heart is a place of quiet contemplation because of time spent with Jesus, I pray that same sense of rest comes upon those who enter my home. As my heart is filled with peace in knowing that God is in control and nothing occurs without His sovereign approval, so too may peace fill my home and be a place for others to find refuge from the storms of this world. Lord, may my home reflect the glorious work that You are doing in my heart. May those who enter my home encounter Your Presence, as I am an extension of Your loving arms. I pray that all the goodness You have poured into me would fill my home and overflow to all who enter in—to Your glory alone. May the spirit of Christmas be felt in my heart and my home not only in December, but all year long. Amen.

Romans 15:13, "May the God of hope fill you with all joy and peace as you trust in him, so that you may overflow with hope by the power of the Holy Spirit."

What are some ways you can carry the warm hope, peace, and joy of the Christmas season with you all year long?

According to Your Word

Luke 1:26-38, "In the sixth month of Elizabeth's pregnancy, God sent the angel Gabriel to Nazareth, a town in Galilee, to a virgin pledged to be married to a man named Joseph, a descendant of David. The virgin's name was Mary. The angel went to her and said, 'Greetings, you who are highly favored! The Lord is with you.' Mary was greatly troubled at his words and wondered what kind of greeting this might be. But the angel said to her, 'Do not be afraid, Mary; you have found favor with God. You will conceive and give birth to a son, and you are to call him Jesus. He will be great and will be called the Son of the Most High. The Lord God will give him the throne of his father David, and he will reign over Jacob's descendants forever; his kingdom will never end.'

'How will this be,' Mary asked the angel, 'since 1 am a virgin?' The angel answered, 'The Holy Spirit will come on you, and the power of the Most High will overshadow you. So the holy one to be born will be called the Son of God.'...

'For nothing will be impossible with God.' And Mary said, 'Behold, I

am the servant of the Lord; let it be to me according to your word.'

And the angel departed from her."

God called Mary to step into the hugest role ever assigned to a human—she was chosen to be the mother to the Son of God. I am so grateful that Mary had the faith to go along with God's plan. The world has been blessed by her obedience.

Following God's directions often leads us to places we would not ordinarily go. Doing the Lord's will is not always easy and often it requires something extraordinary of us. It demands faith and obedience, devotion and trust. It asks us to view the situation through the eyes of God and invites us to see the Lord's mighty Hand at work—both in us and through us. Following the Lord's plan unlocks untold blessings for us and very often everyone around. Following His plan encourages us to step out of our comfort zone and into the wide unknown, where spectacular things are bound to happen. Knowing and believing God enables us to confidently say, *"let it be to me according to Your Word."*

Finish this short prayer with your own request for faith:

Dear Lord, help me confidently and courageously to say, "Let it be to me according to Your Word." Help me to believe that nothing is impossible with You, and move forward in faith...

Amen.

Hand in Hand

Christmas and *love* are tightly woven together, the meaning of each goes hand in hand with the other. The very essence of God is love, and He graciously chose to reveal His gloriously amazing love to us through His Son, Jesus Christ. God's divine love came down to make its home among us on the first blessed Christmas morn. His love arrived on the scene in the form of a baby—His love was humbly born in a stable, nestled and wrapped in a manger. His love was proclaimed by angels above. His love came down from Heaven with the sole purpose of being our Savior. God's extravagant and sacrificial love is the true spirit of Christmas. *Christmas* and *love* cannot be separated; they are absolutely one and the same.

John 3:16-17, "For God so loved the world that he gave his one and only Son, that whoever believes in him shall not perish but have eternal life. For God did not send his Son into the world to condemn the world, but to save the world through him."

How has the love that God showed at Christmas impacted your life?

Continually

My prayer for the New Year is not a *one and done*; it is a prayer I will continue to pray as I greet each and every brand-new day. I pray that my heart would be set on the same desires as the Lord; that my mind would be filled with the same thoughts and focus of Christ; that my eyes would see others with the same compassion and love as Jesus; that my hands would reach out beyond myself, embracing those who come my way; that my feet would follow the footsteps of Christ and the path He has laid out especially for me. I will continually pray that the Lord blesses my year, one precious day at a time.

Psalm 96:2, "Sing to the LORD, praise his name; proclaim his salvation day after day."

Have you considered making prayer a resolution for every day? Today is an excellent day to begin.

Any Time

Worship is not something that just happens within the walls of church. Worship occurs any place and at any time we pause to acknowledge and praise the Lord. This can occur in the car, the shower, on our closet floor, on a walk around the neighborhood, or seated at the ocean's shore. It happens when we lift our eyes above our circumstance and gaze upon His majesty and glory. It takes place any time our hearts find contentment in His Holy Presence. It occurs when we surrender everything over to His loving care. It happens when we raise our hands and sing out loud in adoration, and don't care who's looking because our only concern and focus is completely wrapped up in Him. Whenever and wherever we worship the Lord, the very Spirit of God comes alive in us. Heaven and earth beautifully collide any time our worship joins in with the worship around God's Heavenly Throne.

John 4:23-24, "Yet a time is coming and has now come when the true worshipers will worship the Father in the Spirit and in truth, for they are the kind of worshipers the Father seeks. 24 God is spirit, and his worshipers must worship in the Spirit and in truth."

Where is your most favorite place to worship the Lord? How can you incorporate worship throughout your day?

He Alone

I find comfort and assurance in the arms of my Savior. His love for me reaches higher than the highest heavens and plumbs deeper than the deepest sea. His love pursues and woos and calls to me—from the ends of the earth, He beckons me to make His heart my home. His mercy for me is new every day; He forgives my transgressions and makes me clean. He leads me in the way everlasting and removes my sins far from me. *As far as the east is from the west*—He no longer counts my trespasses against me. His grace over me is abundantly lavish and His blessings upon my life are countless. He carried my sin on His shoulders and bore my shame to the Cross. His blessings for me are quite astounding—I merely ask Jesus to be Lord of my life and He graciously gives me the keys to His Heavenly Kingdom and offers me the hope-filled Promise of being with Him forever.

The Lord's sovereignty over my life is refreshingly boundless. I find great freedom by surrendering control over to Him—I know and believe that my life and this world are in His capable hands. God alone deserves my worship. He alone is worthy of my grateful praise. He alone is the object of my confident faith. He alone is the source of my unshakeable hope. He alone is the wellspring of my unconditional joy!

There is no one like my God and for that I am eternally grateful!

Psalm 86:10, "For you are great and do marvelous deeds;

you alone are God."

Describe who the Lord is to you:

Speechless

There is no one like our God—words merely skim the surface in accurately describing all that He is. The very essence and character of His being leave me speechless and tongue-tied.

God's glory is magnificent and uncontainable. His holiness is lofty and immeasurable. His love is extravagant and unconditional. His mercy is endless and unfathomable. His grace is amazing and uncountable. His power is death-defying and unsurmountable. His righteousness is perfect and unequaled among people.

His radiant glory pervades the heavens and permeates the earth. All of creation testifies and sings His praise. His holiness is the high standard by which we measure our lives, and in response to His holiness we exalt His Name. His love was displayed in its fullness through Jesus' outstretched arms on the Cross. His mercy withholds the judgment our sins deserve—He has paid the penalty for us. Out of gratitude for His mercy toward us, we show undeserved mercy and forgiveness toward others. God's grace is breath-takingly sweet and light, it is amazing to say the least! It is blessing upon blessing poured out on our lives. It is the Lord's goodness that fills us up and overflows to those around. His righteousness made a way for us to be counted as righteous too.

Standing in the Presence of the Lord, we find ourselves at a loss for words. Although we sing His glorious praises, no utterance will completely suffice, so we offer our lives to Him in whole-hearted devotion.

Psalm 150:1-6, "Praise the LORD. Praise God in his sanctuary; praise him in his mighty heavens. Praise him for his acts of power; praise him for his surpassing greatness. Praise him with the sounding of the trumpet, praise him with the harp and lyre, praise him with timbrel and dancing, praise him with the strings and pipe, praise him with the clash of cymbals, praise him with resounding cymbals. Let everything that has breath praise the LORD. Praise the LORD."

What about the Lord astounds you? Take a moment to offer your praise to the Lord here and now:

Love and Blessings

I hope you enjoyed our journey of *worship and wonder* together. I pray that you were *blessed and inspired* along the way.

I pray that you go on to encounter Jesus throughout all your coming days; I hope that you are continually awed and overwhelmed in His Presence and are overcome with uncontainable praise.

In the Name of Jesus, I pray that your hope is unshakable, your joy is uncontainable, God's love floods your heart, and your faith grows bigger every day!

It is with my love and blessings that I close this book.

Xoxo, Tracy

Worship and Wonder

Here is some additional space to write your answers and record any truths that you want to remember. These are your own private pages, just between you and the Lord—so feel free to pour out your heart.

Worship and Wonder

Worship and Wonder

Worship and Wonder

Worship and Wonder

Worship and Wonder

Worship and Wonder

Worship and Wonder

Worship and Wonder

Worship and Wonder

So Grateful...

To Russell, Camden, and Christian. I am grateful to have such amazing men in my life! I am thankful for the huge, unexpected blessing of spending so much of quarantine with all of you under one roof! It was a gift I do not take for granted. Thank you, Camden and Christian, for making my cover so beautiful!

To Ruthie Reese, for being my loving, kind, and faith-filled neighbor. Thank you for taking the time to edit my grammar and punctuation, and delicately refine my words. Thank you for afternoon swims and delightful conversations!

For my new friend Mikhael Armao. I am thankful that God ordained our meeting, bringing us together despite the many miles between us. I love your heart for helping women and how your ministry is providing a haven for them to safely get back on their feet. Your ministry teaches women to find their confidence in the Lord and draw their strength from Him. It also allows them to experience the sweet joy of fellowship with sisters-in-Christ. I know He has big plans for *Worthy Women Ministry,* beyond the borders of Tennessee! I cannot wait to see what He does with your faithful obedience.

Thank you, Lord, for having everything under Your sovereign control, and never leaving or forsaking us!

A Bit About the Author...

First and foremost, I am a woman who loves the Lord with all her heart. I am married to a wonderful man, and I am a mother of two young men (who used to be little boys). I am a daughter, a  sister, a friend, a neighbor. I have a dog, I enjoy taking walks outside, I like chips and salsa, I enjoy traveling, and taking pictures... and my list goes on. I love serving in the women's ministry at my church. I enjoy leading Bible studies and teaching others about the hope, joy, peace, and confidence that is rightfully theirs as children of God. I write to inspire others to deepen their relationships with Jesus through the study of His Word. Even if our lives don't look exactly alike, I'm sure we have plenty in common. We each have ups and downs and face good days and bad. I truly thank you for joining me on this journey and hope that you find encouragement as we seek the Lord together.

Let's connect for some sweet fellowship!

Follow my blog, view video teachings, peek at my other books, and connect with me at: beblessedandinspired.com

Find short and sweet devotions, and connect with me on Facebook at: facebook.com/tracyhillauthor

Additional Inspiration...

More of my titles that are available in stores and online:

A Daughter of the King: Gaining Confidence as a Child of God (A Bible Study): God's desire is for you to discover the confidence and rich blessings of your identity which are found in Jesus Christ. You are loved and forgiven. You belong and matter. You are beautiful and strong, and you have purpose. You are *a Daughter of the King.*

Matthew: Your Kingdom Come (A Bible Study): By studying this amazing Gospel, we will come to know Jesus better and, as a result, fall even more deeply in love with Him. We will hear His teachings, witness His miracles, see His power, feel His love. Encountering Jesus changes our lives forever.

Promise and Possibilities: Hope-Filled Devotions: You will glimpse the promise that life holds and the possibility of all that can be when you place your hope in Jesus. He is truly the One who holds the key.

Confidence and Crowns: Devotions for A Daughter of the King: The devotions, stories, and Scriptures you will encounter, are all intended to point you to the reality of who you are in God's eyes—you are a dearly loved child of God. (The devotions are based on the Bible study, *A Daughter of the King.*)

Lilies and Lemonade: Joy-Filled Devotions: Lilies and Lemonade represents two philosophies which hold the key to optimistic living. A joy-filled perspective is available to us when we look at life with the proper Jesus-filled mindset.

Made in the USA
Columbia, SC
09 November 2021

48577357R00104